Niamh

SECRET
GARDEN

BY FRANCES HODGSON BURNETT
ADAPTED BY JESSICA SWALE

SERVING THEATRE
S F
SINCE 1830

SAMUELFRENCH-LONDON.CO.UK
SAMUELFRENCH.COM

FOR AMATEUR PRODUCTION ENQUIRIES

UNITED KINGDOM AND EUROPE
plays@SamuelFrench-London.co.uk
020 7255 4302/01

UNITED STATES AND CANADA
info@SamuelFrench.com
1-866-598-8449

Each title is subject to availability from Samuel French, depending upon country of performance. Please be aware that *THE SECRET GARDEN* may not be licensed by Samuel French in your territory. Amateur producers should contact the nearest Samuel French office or licensing partner to verify availability.

This adaptation of *The Secret Garden* was first performed on 11th July 2014 at Grosvenor Park Open Air Theatre, Chester in the fifth year of the summer season produced by Chester Performs.

CAST

In order of appearance

MRS PHIPPS .... Hannah Barrie
MARTHA .... Kathryn Delaney
MARY LENNOX..................................... Jessica Clark
MRS LENNOX ....Louise Kempton
AYAH... Kezrena James
MRS MEDLOCK................................. Heather Phoenix
BEN WEATHERSTAFF............................. Gareth Williams
DICKON...Gary Mitchinson
DR CRAVEN.....................................Peter F Gardiner
ARCHIBALD CRAVEN................................. Mark Healy
COLIN CRAVEN .... Max Gallagher

All other roles played by members of the company

CREATIVE TEAM

DIRECTOR.. Kate Saxon
DESIGNER...Jessica Curtis
COMPOSER & MUSIC DIRECTOR ....Sarah Travis
PUPPET DESIGNER & DIRECTOR. ....Toby Olié
LIGHTING DESIGNER.........................Katharine Williams
MOVEMENT DIRECTOR .... Georgina Lamb
DIALECT COACH .... Helen Ashton
CASTING DIRECTOR................................Kay Magson
ASSISTANT DIRECTOR ....Bronagh Lagan

STAGE MANAGEMENT TEAM

COMPANY STAGE MANAGER.......................... Helin Keast
DEPUTY STAGE MANAGER.......................Natalie James-Fox
ASSISTANT STAGE MANAGER .... Kezia Beament
ASSISTANT STAGE MANAGER........................ Laura Smith

FOR CHESTER PERFORMS

PRODUCER...................................... Andrew Bentley
ARTISTIC DIRECTOR ....Alex Clifton

INTRODUCTION

The Secret Garden is a magical tale. It's a story about curiosity and imagination, about children growing up and adults reconnecting with their youths. It is the tale of a thaw, both in the eponymous garden and in the hearts of the characters. And what characters they are. In her novel Hodgson Burnett paints a truly vivid portrait of the spoilt orphan Mary, daughter of British dignitaries in the Raj, who is brought to Misselthwaite Manor when she is orphaned. Used to a life of privilege, in which servants are second class citizens, Mary must overcome her prejudices in order to survive her new life in Yorkshire. And as her horizons broaden, her adventurous spirit grows, and she's soon on a mission to uncover the mysteries of Misselthwaite, the enigma of the crying boy and the location of the Secret Garden.

It is no surprise that *The Secret Garden* is beloved by many generations of readers. It is simultaneously a page turning thriller, a love song to nature and an exploration of grief, passion and the power of curious minds. It has been a joy to adapt.

The play is by no means an exact replica of the book on stage. I have imagined scenarios and changed details in order to tell the tale effectively over the course of an evening in the theatre. Yet I have been faithful to what I believe the spirit and message of a book to be, and in doing so I have come to love the novel even more in my adulthood than I did as a child. I do hope you the journey as much as I have.

A NOTE ON PRODUCTION

Set

This play can be performed by anyone with the passion to do it, regardless of space or budget. The story itself is about creation and invention, and I'm a firm believer in asking the audience to use their imaginations. The stage directions hint at what the story might look like, but they're by no means instructions to be followed to the letter. The carriage in which Mary and Mrs Medlock arrive, for example, could easily be a couple of chairs. If the actors commit to the imaginative journey, the motion of the carriage and the interest of the passing scenery, then the audience will accept it. The references to doors, gates and different rooms are merely a guide to help you visualise the story; they don't need to appear in your set. It's the joy of the magic of theatre; complicated scene changes may well even slow the play down.

In the play's first production, the design team created a garden which grew in and around the furniture of Misselthwaite manor. As the play moves from internal to external, from Winter to Spring, the table and wardrobe of the early scenes were taken over by greenery as the garden came into focus. In this way the whole stage became the garden, and yet the audience still believed in the indoor scenes, as long as the actors did. It's about capturing the spirit of the garden.

PUPPETRY

There's no specific demand here for either a particular kind of puppet, or a great deal of puppetry experience. There are countless ways of making and animating puppets, and it's fun to explore that, whether you wish to populate your production with a whole menagerie of moor animals, or work with the very simplest of gestures. Indeed, it would be perfectly feasible to use a sound effect for the robin, and not have him present at all.

The original production had a puppet lamb, dog, mouse, squirrel and two robins – one 'main robin,' and then the robin 'in flight', who whizzed around on the end of a string. For the most part, they were animated by three puppeteer-actors, who also played the smaller roles. However, at points the actors took over; when Colin has the lamb on his lap, for example.

The greatest lesson I learnt from our marvelous puppet maker Toby Olie is to keep the puppet animated at all times. As soon as he picks up a puppet he makes it breathe. It's captivating, and for that reason it's often preferable to have a separate actor operating a puppet, so that they can take responsibility for keeping it alive. Toby's marvelous creatures can be seen at www.tobyolie.com. You can also look for inspiration to Handspring Puppet Company and the Little Angel Theatre in Islington, London. They do say never work with children or animals, but I'd always make an exception for puppets.

ACKNOWLEDGEMENTS

Thank you to the cast and crew of Chester's Grosvenor Park Theatre, who have turned these pages into a truly enchanting production. Special thank you to Alex Clifton for badgering me to write it, and to Kate Saxon for realising it with so much vision, imagination and patience. Thanks also to the team at Samuel French, to Helen Mumby and the staff at MLR, to Laura Forrest-Hay and Eva Laverty and to Michael Wharley for both beautiful photographs and restorative time out in Brockwell's secret garden. Greatest thanks, of course, to Frances Hodgson Burnett, for her timeless, captivating novel.

For Nell Leyshon
with whom I have dug many weeds
and shared many secrets.

"If you have a garden and a library, that is all you need."
Cicero

"Weeds are flowers too, once you get to know them."
A. A. Milne

The play is set in 1910, in Yorkshire and India.

CHARACTERS

MARY LENNOX – *a young girl*

MARTHA – a servant, *the same age as Mary*

DICKON – *Martha's brother*

COLIN CRAVEN – *a sickly boy*

MRS MEDLOCK – *a strict housekeeper*

ARCHIBALD CRAVEN – *Colin's father (Mary's Uncle)*

BEN WEATHERSTAFF – *the Gardener*

MRS PHIPPS – *a servant at Misselthwaite*

MR PITCHER – *a servant at Misselthwaite*

DR CRAVEN – *Archibald's Cousin*

MRS LENNOX – *Mary's mother*

MR LENNOX – *Mary's father*

AYAH – *the Lennox's Indian house servant*

INSPECTORS 1 AND 2 – *Earthquake experts*

DR MADELEINE BRÉS – *a pioneering Doctor*

Several puppets.

Many of the parts can be doubled.

ACT ONE

Scene One

A Passage from India

(At Misselthwaite Manor, a gaggle of servants are preparing for a new arrival. **MRS PHIPPS** *is folding laundry,* **MARTHA** *is pottering.)*

MARTHA. Mrs Phipps?

MRS PHIPPS. Yes, Martha.

MARTHA. Can I ask you a question?

MRS PHIPPS. Depends.

MARTHA. Depends on what?

MRS PHIPPS. Is it 'Can I help you, Mrs Phipps?'

MARTHA. No.

MRS PHIPPS. Then no. But you can give me a hand. Hold this.

(She gives her the end of a sheet. They fold it together.)

MARTHA. Why're you doing the linen today?

MRS PHIPPS. There's extra to do.

MARTHA. Why is there extra?

MRS PHIPPS. You just hold your tongue and fold; we haven't got long.

MARTHA. Haven't got long before what?

MRS PHIPPS. Before the girl arrives.

MARTHA. What girl?

MRS PHIPPS. You ain't heard? You with your giant ears like bird's wings?

MARTHA. No. Why's she coming here?

1

MRS PHIPPS. She's got nowhere else to go. She's an orphan. And him upstairs is her only relation. She's Mr Craven's niece, though I'm sure he won't want nowt to do with her, for he never sees a soul.

MARTHA. But who is she? And where's she coming from? And what's her name?

MRS PHIPPS. If I tell ya, will you stop asking questions?

MARTHA. Yes.

MRS PHIPPS. She's coming from India. And her name is Mary Lennox.

MARTHA. Mary Lennox?

MRS LENNOX. *(Off)* Mary Lennox!!

(Misselthwaite transforms into India, as MRS LENNOX *arrives with all the glamour of the Raj. The servants transform into members of the Indian household. It is a busy hubbub – the preparation for a party.* MARY LENNOX *climbs out of the laundry basket and hides on one side of it.)*

MRS LENNOX. Mary! Mary Lennox! Where is that petulant child? Hey you! Where's my daughter?

AYAH. Ma'am, I don't know.

MRS LENNOX. Well go and find her, useless woman. Mary? Mary!

*(*AYAH *rushes off in search of* MARY, *who is hiding behind the laundry basket.* MARY *sneaks round it whilst her mother goes the other way – she makes a run for it. Too late.)*

Mary Lennox. Where do you think you're going?! Hey! Look at me when I'm talking to you. I asked you where you were going.

MARY. To see the pangolin.

MRS LENNOX. The what?

MARY. The pangolin. It's a kind of scaly anteater. He lives in the papaya trees.

MRS LENNOX. I don't give a flea where he lives – it's a filthy animal. I thought we told you not to play outside.

MARY. But there's no-one to play with inside.

MRS LENNOX. Precisely, now why don't – *(realising)* wait... who exactly were you playing with outside?

MARY. Raman.

MRS LENNOX. Raman?

MARY. He's my friend. He lives in the yellow hut.

MRS LENNOX. A native?!

MARY. He's teaching me how to play Kichi Kichi Thambalam. It's where you bury a stick in the sand and the other person has to dig it up –

MRS LENNOX. Mary Lennox! What have I told you about playing with dirty natives in dirty sandpits? I really don't know why you feel the need to play at all. Good children don't play, they sit in silence. *(To* AYAH*)* Ayah, this is your doing. You let her out.

AYAH. No, ma'am.

MRS LENNOX. You must have done.

AYAH. On my life, I didn't.

MRS LENNOX. Mary, come here. Did you sneak out like a little devil or is Ayah lying to me? One of you is a liar. And you know what we do with liars, don't you?

MARY. We beat them.

MRS LENNOX. Yes, we beat them. Mary, you wouldn't let me down would you? Not after all the money we've spent on you. All your dresses...and shoes...and your expensive education. You know mummy won't love you if you've lied. Who's the liar, Mary? Mary?

MARY. *(Pause)* It was Ayah.

AYAH. Miss Mary!

MRS LENNOX. Good girl.

AYAH. Ma'am, please, I swear –

MRS LENNOX. You can't be trusted with anything. Get out.

AYAH. But Ma'am –

MRS LENNOX. You're done here. We'll find someone else.

AYAH. I'm not a liar.

(**MRS LENNOX** *slaps* **AYAH.**)

MRS LENNOX. Don't' contradict me! You're nothing but a filthy native. What is she, Mary?

(**MARY** *won't answer.*)

Mary!!

MARY. A filthy native.

MRS LENNOX. And what do we when we're disobeyed?

(**MARY** *slaps* **AYAH.**)

MRS LENNOX. *(To* **AYAH***)* You're done here.

AYAH. But my children! How will I keep them?

MRS LENNOX. You should have thought of that before.

AYAH. There's nowhere else to work.

MRS LENNOX. That's not my concern.

AYAH. How will we live?! My children!

(She goes to exit, then rallies herself to speak to her Mistress.)

Perhaps if you loved your own child, you'd understand what it means to be a mother.

MRS LENNOX. Get out! Out!

(**AYAH** *leaves.*)

Now, what do you think of my dress? I was going to wear the russet gown with the silk brocade, but I think I look thinner in this. Do you think your father will like it? Mary? What's wrong with you? Is this about Ayah?

(Mary looks down.)

(Softening) Mary, what have we told you? There are two types of people in the world. Proper people, like us, and serving people, like Ayah. And when they don't behave, it's our duty to punish them. Do you understand?

MARY. Yes Mama.

(**MARY** *suddenly hugs her mother. She comforts her rather awkwardly.*)

MRS LENNOX. Alright, alright. Now let me get ready.

MARY. *(Pause)* May I come to the party?

MRS LENNOX. No. Children should be seen and not heard.

MARY. So can I come if I'm quiet?

MRS LENNOX. What?

MARY. You said children should be seen.

MRS LENNOX. When did I say that?

MARY. You said children should be seen / and not heard.

MRS LENNOX. You're imagining things again! Now go to your room and sit in silence. Or... read the bible or something.

MARY. But –

MRS LENNOX. You are not to speak again. Not another single word 'til I say so –

MARY. But please –

MRS LENNOX. Mary! *(Pause)* That's better. Oh, Robert darling! Do I look fabulous?

(Her husband has arrived, looking suave and ball – ready. She gives him a twirl.)

MR LENNOX. You look radiant. Like the jewel in the crown, don't you think, Mary? Mary?

MRS LENNOX. She's not allowed to speak. She's been lying.

MR LENNOX. Has she indeed? You know what we do with liars, Mary. We feed them to the crocodiles.

MRS LENNOX. Snap, snap, snap!

MR LENNOX. Now, we mustn't keep them waiting, darling.

MRS LENNOX. No, indeed. I want to make the most of my entrance. Mary, go to your room. And remember, not a word until I say.

*(**MARY** nods and moves away as loud Indian music signals the beginning of the party. It is a spectacular burst of exotic delights. **MRS LENNOX** gets a round of*

applause as she sweeps into the scene with her elegant dress. MARY *sneaks in and edges her way around, always making sure that she keeps out of her mother's eye line. When her mother sashays towards her in a dance with her father,* MARY *dives inside the laundry basket. Then a rumble, the music distorts and the whole scene is destroyed by a devastating earthquake. Everything is thrown about, broken, like dolls shattering against each other. Utter destruction, fading to silence. Time passes. Nothing moves. Two inspectors arrive to survey the wreckage as if several days later.)*

INSPECTOR 1. Lord above. Look at this place.

INSPECTOR 2. Three hundred feet West of the epicentre. I'm surprised there's anything left at all.

INSPECTOR 1. You know, it was one of the most beautiful buildings in Manipur. I came to a party here once.

INSPECTOR 2. *You* got an invite?!

INSPECTOR 1. Don't sound so surprised.

INSPECTOR 2. Well. Good job they never asked you back – you'd have ended up in the dust like the rest of them.

INSPECTOR 1. Such a waste.

INSPECTOR 2. Were there any survivors?

INSPECTOR 1. Only one – A servant. She'd been dismissed by the Lady of the house just hours before the quake – it broke her heart to be sent away, but it seems it saved her life. She was nursemaid to the little girl.

INSPECTOR 2. There was a girl?

INSPECTOR 1. Mary Lennox. An odd little thing by all accounts.

INSPECTOR 2. You met her?

INSPECTOR 1. Oh no, they kept her out of sight. Her parents were too steeped in gin to pay her much attention. Most people never even knew they had a child. She wouldn't have stood a chance.

INSPECTOR 2. Can we get out of here, I don't like it.

INSPECTOR 1. Let's take a look outside.

(As they turn to go, behind them the laundry basket opens up and **MARY** *emerges, shell shocked, covered in dust. She coughs. The inspectors turn round and can't believe their eyes.)*

INSPECTOR 1. Bloody Nora, what on earth?

INSPECTOR 2. It's her. The girl.

INSPECTOR 1. Mary? Are you Mary Lennox?

*(***MARY*** can't speak. She just nods in a daze. The two men walk to her and lift her up. A musical sequence in which she is helped, mended, cleaned, redressed, packed off with a coat, hat and suitcase…)*

MAN. Mary. Mary Lennox? You're to go to England.

*(***MARY*** goes to England.)*

Scene Two

Misselthwaite Manor

(**MARY** *is on a carriage with* **MRS MEDLOCK**, *Misselthwaite's housekeeper, travelling across the moor towards Misselthwaite Manor.*)

MRS MEDLOCK. Sandwich?

(**MARY** *shakes her head.*)

You sure? Corned beef and spring onions?

(**MARY** *looks away.* **MRS MEDLOCK** *begins to unwrap one for herself.*)

Well, you're going to be wondrous company, aren't you. I am glad we have six hours journeying together without another soul on the horizon. Well if you shan't talk, you'll have to listen, for you ought to know something of where we're going; it's a far cry from what you're used to, I'm sure. Misselthwaite Manor is six hundred years old and it belongs to your Uncle. There's near a hundred rooms in it though most of them's shut up and locked. And there's portraits and tapestries and dark old furniture, and chimneys that smoke and gardens which stretch to the moor's edge. But apart from that, there's nothing. Nothing at all. Why they're bringing you here I don't know, for it's no place for a child. Mr Craven won't want to be troubled by you, that's for sure.

(*The carriage arrives and the staff are assembled. They watch* **MARY** *as she approaches.*)

MARTHA. Is that her? Mary Lennox?

MRS PHIPPS. I've never seen such a marred looking young 'un in my life.

MRS MEDLOCK. *(Getting out of the carriage)* Ah, Mr Pitcher.

MR PITCHER. Mrs Medlock.

MRS MEDLOCK. What did his Lordship say?

MR PITCHER. He said you are to take her to her room. He doesn't want to see her. He's going to London in the morning.

MRS MEDLOCK. Very well. So long as I know what's expected of me.

MR PITCHER. What's expected of you is to make sure he doesn't see what he doesn't want to see.

MRS MEDLOCK. Right. Well then, Mary. Say how do you do to Mr Pitcher.

*(**MARY** says nothing.)*

You're not going to be a rude little madam, are you? You ought to be grateful that you've anywhere to live at all.

MR PITCHER. Seems she doesn't deserve for him to see her anyhow.

*(**MARY** turns away sadly.)*

MRS MEDLOCK. There's nowt to be done with her. Martha take her to her room. See if you can make her talk. The rest of you, back to work.

*(The scene transforms into **MARY**'s bedroom. She stands silently with her suitcase, dressed in hat, coat, etc. It is late morning.)*

MARTHA. Miss. I'm Martha Sowerby. I'm to be tha maid. Good to meet you.

*(**MARY** says nothing.)*

I like tha shoes. And tha hat. And tha face.

*(**MARY** says nothing.)*

Why don't you speak? Can't you speak? You got no tongue in your mouth? Or do you just not want to speak? *(Pause)* Fair enough. Let us take your case.

(She steps towards **MARY**. **MARY** *steps away immediately. It's like a game of cat and mouse.)*

Or your coat?

(She takes another step forward, **MARY** *steps away.)*

Well, I say. Look, you don't have to talk to me. Maybe I'll just leave thee to be quiet by thyself. Tis a shame though, for...well I wasn't going to say anything, but I have a mighty big secret to tell, and I have no-one to tell it to. I did think tha looked just the sort that might like to know a big shiny secret, but if you don't want to know, I shall just have to keep it to meself. Keep it quiet and go to my grave with it. Tis such a waste, for it is the best secret I ever heard, but nay matter. I shall come back to turn the bed later. *(Going)* Eh what a big secret it is, but I shall just have to tell / Dickon instead –

MARY. What's the secret?! *(She immediately covers her mouth with her hands)*

MARTHA. Ha ha! I knew tha could talk, I knew it! They all said tha couldn't speak but I said that's hog swill –

MARY. What's the secret?

MARTHA. Well I can't just tell thee.

MARY. Why not?

MARTHA. Not without our being proper friends first.

(She puts her hand out for **MARY** *to shake.* **MARY** *doesn't.)*

Won't you shake my hand?

MARY. No.

MARTHA. Why not?

MARY. We can't be friends.

MARTHA. We can.

MARY. We can't. You're a servant.

MARTHA. Strange how tha doesn't talk for hours then when tha does, tha says such a funny thing.

MARY. There are two types of people – proper people and serving people. Proper people only talk to serving people to give them their orders.

MARTHA. Oh. Well that is a shame, for serving people most often know all the best secrets, and other things that are fascinating and curious, that proper people would love to know if only they took their noses out of the air.

MARY. You can't say that!

MARTHA. You just said I wasn't a proper person. What makes you more proper than me?

MARY. My father was the Viceroy of India. Who's yours?

MARTHA. He's a tanner. He lives on the scarp with me mam and my seven sisters. And my brother, Dickon, he can talk to animals.

MARY. No-one can talk to animals.

MARTHA. Dickon can. He tames them. They follow him around like he's dropping crumbs, but he an't. He's just got a way with 'em.

MARY. Is he a fakir?

MARTHA. A what?

MARY. A snake charmer.

MARTHA. Not just snakes. Badgers, lapwings, hares.

MARY. He can't tame hairs.

MARTHA. Why not?

MARY. He's not a hairbrush.

MARTHA. No! Hares what are like rabbits, but with longer ears and quicker legs. Ain't you never heard of a hare before?

MARY. Of course I've heard of a hare! Don't laugh at me, you filthy native.

MARTHA. I beg your pardon.

MARY. Your parents are no-one, they're nobody!

MARTHA. Course they are. Without 'em I'd just be air on the moor.

MARY. They're nobodies!

MARTHA. You're only saying that cos yours are dead.

(A stand off. **MARY** *might cry if she wasn't so stubborn. Instead, she runs for the door.)*

MARTHA. Mary! Mary! I didn't mean...

(But she's gone.)

Scene Three

Winter Gardens

(**MARY** *is storming through the garden in a foul mood. She doesn't know where she's going. There's a robin, singing in a tree on the other side of the wall.*)

MARY. Stupid bird, be quiet!

(*The robin stops singing, then, after a pause, whistles back a cocky – sounding response.* **MARY** *stops in her tracks. She looks at the robin suspiciously. The robin tweets, as if he's laughing.*)

You're laughing at me too!

(*He sings again.* **MARY** *picks up a stone and throws it at the robin, who flies up and away.* **MARY** *continues on her angry march through the garden, and comes across an old man,* **BEN WEATHERSTAFF**. **MARY** *is wary of* **BEN**.)

BEN. Eh up lass.

(**MARY** *doesn't say anything.*)

What's wrong with thee? Don't they teach you introductions where tha comes from?

MARY. No.

BEN. Not from round here, are ya?

MARY. No.

BEN. That all you can say is it, 'No'?

MARY. No.

BEN. Well I say. What a little crab apple thou art.

MARY. I am not. (*Pause*) What's a crab apple?

13

BEN. Tha'd know if thee bit one. You'd spit it out straightways. What you doing wandering down here any road?

MARY. Just looking. What is this place?

BEN. One of the kitchen gardens.

MARY. And what's that?

BEN. Another one. And then another on t'other side. And another on t'other. They look bare as an egg now, but when the spring comes...

(The robin arrives, singing, and sits in a tree.)

Eh, look. Where's thou been, tha cheeky beggar? Courting this early in the season? Thou art too forward, I tell thee!

*(**BEN** whistles and the robin replies.)*

BEN. See that, he talks to me.

MARY. How did you make him do that?

BEN. I don't make him. We've been friends since he was a fledgling. He fell out of his nest, see. So I nursed him better. But by the time he was strong enough to fly back, his folks had all gone. So now he's got me instead. We have each other.

MARY. What sort of bird is he?

BEN. Doesn't thou know? Why he's a robin red breast. Oh look, he likes it when ya talk about him. Show off.

*(**MARY** steps nearer to the robin.)*

Why don't tha try whistling to him?

MARY. No.

BEN. No?

MARY. I don't know how.

BEN. Eh, he could teach you.

*(The Robin whistles at **MARY**.)*

Eh, dang me if he hasn't taken a fancy to thee.

MARY. Why would he do that?

BEN. Lord only knows, for tha'rt given him no reason. Speak to him, go on.

MARY. *(Nonplussed)* Hello bird.

BEN. Eh! Not so gruff. Put your hand out, and speak soft so's tha don't scare him.

(**MARY** *puts her hand out. Very slowly and cautiously, the robin begins to hop towards her.*)

MARY. *(Softly)* Hello. Hello bird. *(To* **BEN**, *annoyed)* He's not coming!

BEN. Go gently.

MARY. *(Gently)* Come on bird. Come on.

(The robin jumps onto **MARY**'*s hand. She bats him off, disgusted and he flies off.*)

Ugh!! Get off!

BEN. Hey! You'll never make a friend of him like that, you're sharp as an old stick. You must speak to him as Dickon does, kindly and soft.

MARY. You know Dickon?

BEN. Everybody knows Dickon. The very blackberries and heather bell knows him. I'll warrant the foxes shows him where their cubs lie, and the wren don't hide their nests from him.

(The robin chirps at her, then takes off and darts about.)

MARY. Where's he going?

BEN. He never stays for long.

MARY. He's flying back to the garden on the other side of the wall.

BEN. That's where his nest is.

MARY. How do you get there?

BEN. Hey, don't you go poking your nose around where it's not wanted. You stick to the path. Eh! Where are you going?

(**MARY**'*s gone.*)

Sour little crab apple.

(**MARY** *follows the robin but he's too quick for her.*)

MARY. Hey! Come back! Come back! Why does no-one do
what I say!

Scene Four

Hints of a Thaw

(**MARY** *and* **MARTHA** *are in* **MARY***'s bedroom.*)

MARTHA. Here, Mrs Medlock says you're to change out of those old things.

MARY. I don't want to.

MARTHA. You can have 'em back once they're washed. I'll press 'em for you. I'll do 'em nice. With spray! Please?

MARY. If you tell me the secret.

MARTHA. What secret?

MARY. The shiny one.

MARTHA. Oh. *(Pause)* Mary, I really shouldn't have –

MARY. Then I shan't change.

MARTHA. *(Pause)* Alright, I'll tell thee. But only if you change first.

(**MARY** *puts her arms out expectantly.*)

What are you doing?

MARY. You said I was to change.

MARTHA. Aye.

MARY. Well then. Undress me.

MARTHA. You can't do it yourself?

MARY. It's your job.

(**MARTHA** *starts laughing.*)

Don't laugh at me!

MARTHA. Eh, I meant no harm. Here, put tha arms up. Take hold of the hem and pull!

(MARTHA helps MARY change. MARY gets the dress stuck over her head.)

MARY. I'm stuck!

MARTHA. Pull!

MARY. I can't!

(MARY pops through.)

MARTHA. See! Was that too hard? Here you are. Look!

(She takes some clothes out.)

MARY. They're not mine. Mine are black.

MARTHA. The Master's orders. He won't have thee moping around in mourning making the place even sadder. Mrs Medlock bought 'em 'specially.

MARY. But they're not mine. My mother always chooses mine!

(Suddenly MARY gets upset, though she's desperate for MARTHA not to see.)

MARTHA. Mary?

(MARY is upset and moves away.)

Mary? *(Pause)* You must miss em. I can't imagine it, not having me Mam. Here.

(MARTHA hands her a handkerchief and MARY takes it. MARTHA tries to cheer her up with a new dress.)

Eh, look at this one. Fancy having a dress all to thaself, and not having to share it.

(She helps MARY into the dress.)

Look at you. Th'art white as a goose and tha's eaten nothing since tha got here.

MARY. I'm not hungry.

MARTHA. You'll never get hungry whilst you mope around. You need to run and breathe and lark about, like Dickon does. Then you'll have an appetite.

(Elsewhere, DICKON emerges on the moor. He takes out a pipe whistle and starts to play.)

MARY. What's the secret? *(Pause)* You promised!

MARTHA. You swear you won't breathe a word.

MARY. I swear.

MARTHA. Swear on tha heart. On tha life.

MARY. I swear.

MARTHA. Once, years ago, your Uncle was married, to the most sweet natured creature. They loved each other like swans do, I swear he'd have chased half way round the earth to pick her a blade of grass if she'd asked. She loved the open air, and the moor, and one Summer she built a garden. From a patch of mud she raised the most wondrous place; cowslips and lilacs, fox gloves and blue bells. It was like Eden, so they said. And they'd go inside and read together, talk and sing and caper about. For her birthday, he built her a swing, with honeysuckle wound round the ropes of it. But then, in the Autumn, when a chill was in the air... one day the ropes snapped, and she fell. And though the doctor came straightways, no-one could save her. And since that day the house has been cold. He had the garden locked up and he buried the key. That was ten years hence, and now there's not a soul, save the Master himself, who knows where the garden is or where the key is buried.

MARY. But there must be a door?

MARTHA. None has ever seen it.

MARY. I want to go there.

MARTHA. You can't! You must forget I ever told you. It's not to be spoken of. Not the garden, nor the lady.

MARY. What was her name?

MARTHA. Lilias Craven.

MARY. She was my aunt. My mother's twin. I didn't know.

(MARY and MARTHA look at each other. DICKON begins to sing. As he does, a fox appears and sits by him, followed by a squirrel. DICKON sings for the entranced animals. During the song MARY goes out into the garden and comes across DICKON. She hides and listens.)

SONG 1: SONG OF THE MOOR

TONGUE TIED IS THE SKY LARK
BUT HIS SONG, TIED TO THE BRIGHT ARC
OF THE WIND,
WHISTLES PAST THE BRISTLE CUP
AND THISTLES, UP AND DOWN.

NO WORDS HAS THE MOOR HEN,
OR NIGHT OWL ON A ROCKY FEN
BUT IN SONG,
HOW HE SPEAKS UPON THE AIR,
AND WEARS A TAWNY CROWN.

MOORLAND OF THE MINSTRELS,
MISTLETHRUSH AND KESTREL,
SONG OF HAWK AND HONEY BEE,
MELODY, HARMONY.
VOICES OF THE MOORLAND,
FIN AND FEATHER WHISTLE BAND,
UNDER VALE AND OVER TOR,
SONG OF THE MOOR.

Scene Five

Dickon

(As the song draws to a close, **DICKON** *turns around and spots* **MARY.** *She's mortified that she's been caught.)*

DICKON. Were ya spying on me?

MARY. No. I was watching the animals.

(He whistles again and the robin appears and flies down to sit on his shoulder.)

DICKON. Look. Magic.

MARY. You're Dickon?!

DICKON. And you're Miss Mary.

MARY. How do you know?

DICKON. I know all about you.

MARY. What have they told you? That I don't like to speak and I haven't any friends, I suppose?

DICKON. You do have a friend, look. *(He indicates the robin)*

MARY. He doesn't like me.

DICKON. He does! He told me.

MARY. I don't believe you.

DICKON. Don't then.

*(***MARY*** moves and* **DICKON** *puts his arm out to stop her.)*

DICKON. Eh! Don't tha move! Look.

*(***MARY*** slowly turns back round, and sees there is a squirrel, standing cautiously nearby.* **DICKON** *begins to play on his pipe and the squirrel stands, watching him and might take a couple of steps towards* **DICKON.** **MARY** *takes a step towards it, which spooks it. The squirrel runs off.)*

MARY. None of them like me!

DICKON. Hey, you gotta move slow, that's all. Tha must be gentle and speak low when wild things are about. It's only cos you don't know 'em yet. Do you like it, playing out here? Better than being inside.

MARY. I'm not playing.

DICKON. You are.

MARY. I'm not. Good children don't play. Especially outside. Especially with boys.

DICKON. What's wrong with boys?

MARY. They're dirty. Mother said.

DICKON. Girls and boys are just the same, no real difference, 'cept boys have dangly bits.

MARY. Dickon!

DICKON. What? It's what we're made of, isn't it?

MARY. It's rude!

DICKON. You're rude.

MARY. How am I rude?

DICKON. Rude to God.

MARY. What?

DICKON. Yep. God made us, all of us, including the bits that stick out and the bits that speak and the bits that dangle. So if you say them dangly bits are rude, you're saying God's rude, and that's rude to God.

(The robin chirps.)

Eh, he does like you. You should be chuffed, for he's a choosy little blighter.

MARY. Where does he live?

DICKON. Yonder.

MARY. Yonder where?

DICKON. Beyond the trees.

MARY. Beyond the trees where? *(Taking a risk)* In the secret garden?

DICKON. Eh, how dost thou know about that?!

MARY. Do you know where it is, or how to get in?

DICKON. No. But I should like to. More than anything.

MARY. Why 'more than anything'?

DICKON. When a garden's kept proper, like these, all weeded and neat, that chases the wild away. But when it's left alone, for nature, who knows what secret things 'ud grow there. Imagine what cubs and nippers might be born amongst them roots.

MARY. Spose.

DICKON. Spose? That all you gotta say? That was my big speech.

(MARY nods.)

Not got many words, have ya. You're quiet, like a plover. Martha said you wouldn't say owt when you got here. Were you scared to speak?

MARY. No.

DICKON. So why didn't you?

MARY. Why should I tell you?

DICKON. Cos I like thee. *(Indicating the robin)* So does he.

MARY. My Mother told me not to speak. She said I wasn't to speak until she told me I could. And then she…that was before…

DICKON. I don't suppose she meant forever. Eh, listen, I'll make a bargain with thee. If I find the garden, I'll take thee. If you don't tell.

MARY. I wouldn't tell.

DICKON. And you must take me, if you find it.

MARY. *(Pause)* Alright.

DICKON. We must shake on it.

(He puts his hand out. She doesn't want to take it.)

Go on. Eh, don't embarrass me in front of him *(the robin)* or I'll never hear the end of it.

*(This makes **MARY** smile. They shake hands, albeit reluctantly on her part.)*

(Cut to **DR CRAVEN** *and* **MRS MEDLOCK** *in conversation, en route to see* **COLIN**.*)*

DR CRAVEN. How is the invalid?

MRS MEDLOCK. I'm afraid there's no improvement.

DR CRAVEN. Have you done as I instructed?

MRS MEDLOCK. Yes Sir.

DR CRAVEN. Exactly as I told you? Kept his calipers tight and his braces locked?

MRS MEDLOCK. Of course, Doctor.

DR CRAVEN. We'll see. Take me to him.

(Exeunt.)

Scene Six

Gaining an Appetite

(An evening a short while later. In **MARY**'s *room. It is raining. She is eating.)*

MARY. Will the rain ever stop?

MARTHA. We're in Yorkshire. So probably not.

MARY. It's boring when it rains. You can't go outside.

MARTHA. I thought tha hated the outside.

*(***MARTHA*** smiles to herself.* **MARY** *finishes her supper.)*

MARY. Finished.

MARTHA. Well I never, clean as a sink! You'll be asking for seconds soon.

MARY. There's nothing to do when it rains.

MARTHA. Can tha knit?

MARY. No.

MARTHA. Can tha sew?

MARY. No.

MARTHA. Can tha read?

MARY. Everyone can read.

MARTHA. I can't.

MARY. Can't you? *(Pause)* Maybe I could read to you?

MARTHA. Would tha?

MARY. You shouldn't be stupid all your life.

MARTHA. Thanks very much! *(Kindly)* I should like that.

MARY. We haven't any books.

MARTHA. There's hundreds here. If Mrs Medlock would unlock the library.

MARY. Everything's locked. Why did Mr Craven lock up the garden?

MARTHA. Eh, I told you, you mustn't talk of it.

MARY. But it was her garden and he loved her, why would he shut it up?

(The wind howls. A child's cry rides on the wind.)

MARY. What was that?

MARTHA. What?

MARY. I heard a cry.

MARTHA. You didn't.

(Pause. Silence. Then the cry again.)

MARY. There!

MARTHA. You imagined it.

MARY. Everyone always says I'm imagining but I'm not!

(Suddenly the light is blown out and the cry returns.)

MARY. It is someone crying and it isn't a grown up!

MARTHA. It was just the wind, and if it wasn't it was Mrs Phipps, for she's had toothache all day.

*(**MARY** sees a mouse scuttle across the floor.)*

MARY. Argh!

MARTHA. What?

MARY. A thing. A thing, with a tail. And a snout and all grey. Look, there!

*(The mouse scuttles past. **MARY** is terrified. **MARTHA** spots an opportunity.)*

MARTHA. Mary! 'Tis a wildeebeast[1]!

MARY. A what?!

MARTHA. A man munching, child crunching wildeebeast, the most fearsome creature on the moor. They sneak in at night in packs and when you're asleep they climb upon your hair and bite your neck off.

---

[1] Pronounced with all three syllables, 'wild – *ee* – beast', with 'ee' as in bee. Not as in a 'wildebeest,' the African mammal.

MARY. Get it out of here! Get it out, get it out!

*(**MARY** throws things at it and tries to swat it.)*

MARTHA. Stop, stop! *(Laughing)* It's just a mouse.

MARY. A what?

MARTHA. You must know what a mouse is.

MARY. We didn't have mouses in India. Do they really bite your neck off?

MARTHA. No.

MARY. But they are dangerous?

MARTHA. Only if you were a crumb of cheese. *(Pause.* **MARY***'s not convinced).* Come on, I was just jesting with thee.

(The mouse emerges again and squeaks.)

MARY. You tricked me.

MARTHA. I was joking! Don't be crabby, especially not with him. He might even make friends with thee if you save him some cheese from your supper. Now I must fetch your blankets or tha' never get to bed.

*(**MARTHA** exits. The mouse scuttles off.* **MARY** *thinks for a minute, then takes a piece of left over cheese from her plate and puts it on the floor.)*

MARY. Where are you? Come here. Oh wildeebeast.

(Nothing. She tries whistling, like she did with the robin. It doesn't work.)

Oh! Ee eee!

(The little mouse appears. He's very cautious. **MARY** *nudges the piece of cheese closer towards him. He comes a little closer. He squeaks. She answers. He squeaks again and gets a little closer. She squeaks again. They sit and look at each other. Then he grabs the piece and disappears under a tapestry hanging on the wall.)*

Hey. Hey! Where've you gone? Wait...

(She pushes. The tapestry moves. It is a secret door.)

Hey, wait for me!

(*Music.* **MARY** *follows the mouse down a maze of corridors. It's dark and scary and the corridors seem to be changing around her.*)

Mr Wildeebeast?! Mr Wildeebeast! Where are you? I don't know the way back!

(*Just then she hears a child cry. It's very close by. She freezes. Another cry. She heads towards it and walks straight into* **MRS MEDLOCK**.)

MRS MEDLOCK. What do you think you're doing here? I've told you you're not to wander around the house.

MARY. But I heard crying.

MRS MEDLOCK. No you didn't.

MARY. I heard a boy crying.

MRS MEDLOCK. Don't lie.

MARY. I'm not lying!

(*The sound of a cry from behind the door.*)

MARY. There!

MRS MEDLOCK. I didn't hear anything.

(*The cry happens again.* **MRS MEDLOCK** *tries to cover it (badly) with a weird throat noise. A beat.* **MARY** *looks at her.*)

Bless me! What a terrible cold has come upon me.

(*The cry happens again.* **MRS MEDLOCK** *does a similarly terrible comic cover up.*)

MARY. You're coughing on purpose.

MRS MEDLOCK. I'm doing nothing of the sort! Now back to your room. And if I catch you up here again I shall lock you in your room.

(**MRS MEDLOCK** *jangles her keys at* **MARY** *and* **MARY** *runs away.*)

Hey, hey! I haven't finished with you!

Scene Seven

A Present for Mary

(MARY *is in her room with* MARTHA.)

MARY. Where were you yesterday? Mrs Phipps made my supper; it wasn't as good as when you do it.

MARTHA. It was my day off.

MARY. Oh. What did you do?

MARTHA. I went home, of course. Dickon and I walked all the way across the scarp, and the skylarks played above us like they were dancing to a jig. Then we made dough cakes with bits of brown sugar, and sat round the table and talked.

MARY. What about?

MARTHA. Stories of a young sprite who'd come all the way from India.

MARY. They're not interested in me.

MARTHA. They are. Our Lizzie thinks you're a princess. And Ma nearly fainted clean away when I told her you'd had a tiger in your garden – though she was put out that you're left by yourself with no governess, no nurse and no mother to look after you. So we said we must do our best to cheer thee up.

MARY. You always cheer me up. You speak funny.

MARTHA. You speak funny. I speak Yorkshire.

MARY. That tha do.

MARTHA. Mary! Here, close tha eyes.

MARY. Why?

MARTHA. For a present.

MARY. A present?

MARTHA. Yes indeed.

MARY. But you're poor!

MARTHA. We all agreed tuppence from my wages to buy thee summat was right and proper. We've got more than we need, a fire to warm us, and each other for company. It's not fair that some people have all the good things. Go on. Close your eyes.

(MARY *closes her eyes.* MARTHA *puts a skipping rope in* MARY*'s hand. When* MARY *opens her eyes she almost cries.*)

Mary, don't you like it?

MARY. It's the best present I've ever had. What is it?

MARTHA. Didn't they have skipping ropes in India? Look here, you put one handle in each hand and skip.

(MARY *tries. She is rubbish.*)

You got to keep the rope tight and swing it. I'll show you.

(MARTHA *shows her. She is a skipping machine.* MARY *is captivated and laughs.* MARTHA *shows off and sings a skipping song as she skips.*)

(*Singing*)

"AN ANT AND A FLEA WENT OUT TO SEA,
UPON A REEL OF COTTON,
THE ANT WAS DROWNED BUT THE FLEA WAS FOUND,
BITING A LADIES BOTTOM!"

MARY. (*Amused*) Martha! You can't say that!

MARTHA. I did though, didn't I!

MARY. Where did you learn a rhyme like that?

MARTHA. Mrs Medlock taught me.

MARY. She never did!

MARTHA. Of course she didn't. I don't spose she's ever said 'bottom' in her life. Eh, your turn. Just think of some words what rhyme together.

MARY. *(Taking the rope and skipping slowly, getting better as she goes)* I think I've got one.

MARTHA. Is it rude?

MARY. It might be.

(Singing)

A MAN AND A LADY,
WENT TO CHURCH,
TO JOIN TOGETHER IN WEDLOCK.
BUT THE FELLOW WENT PALE
WHEN HE LIFTED HER VEIL,
FOR UNDER IT WAS MRS MEDLOCK!"

(Both girls fall about laughing. Then MARTHA stops suddenly and straights herself up. MARY notices, and turns round, only to find MRS MEDLOCK standing in the doorway holding a pile of books.)

MARY. Mrs Medlock – I didn't see you.

MRS MEDLOCK. Evidently not. I'd brought you some books from the library but it seems you're quite capable of making your own entertainment.

MARY. Please may I have a book? I want to read it to Martha.

MRS MEDLOCK. Martha's got sheets to wash. *(To MARTHA)* Get out of here.

MARTHA. Yes ma'am. *(She goes)*

MRS MEDLOCK. And you. Out!

MARY. Sorry Mrs / Medlock.

MRS MEDLOCK. Out! And take that ridiculous toy with you before I wrap it around your neck.

(MARY runs out. MRS MEDLOCK is left for a moment on her own. She is hurt. Then she pulls herself together and walks out.)

Scene Eight

Weeds

(**MARY** *goes out into the garden and skips around, improving as she goes. As she skips through the gardens.* **BEN WEATHERSTAFF** *arrives unseen, and scoops the unwitting* **MARY** *up into his wheelbarrow.*)

BEN. Hey, what's this then? Tha's a funny looking weed for me to put in the composting.

MARY. Martha bought me a skipping rope.

BEN. Did she now? Well I think that makes you the luckiest weed I've ever met.

MARY. I'd like to be a weed.

BEN. You are an odd 'un. Most lasses would like to be a cowslip, or a primrose, or summat sweet smelling, but you'd be an old piece of crabgrass, would ya? Or a ragwort?

MARY. Weeds are wild. They can do as they choose. When a garden's kept properly, all the wild's chased away – but if it's left to itself, that's the best. That's what Dickon said.

BEN. Well, Dickon needs get a clip round the ear talking like that, for he'll have me out of a job.

MARY. What would you be, if you could be a plant?

BEN. I don't know. What doest tha think?

MARY. I think you'd be a rataloo.

BEN. I beg your pardon?

MARY. It's a vegetable from India.

BEN. A vegetable? *(Tipping her out of the barrow)* Well thank you very much.

MARY. Some people call them elephant's feet cos they're big and rough looking –

BEN. Now you watch it –

MARY. But inside they are delicious. They're a bit like you, Mr Weatherstaff.

BEN. What, 'cause I'm hardy on the outside but soft underneath?

MARY. No. 'Cause they're bumpy and muddy and have funny stumpy hairy bits.

BEN. You!

MARY. Come on, you have to choose. What would you be?

BEN. A potato.

MARY. Why?

BEN. Cos then I could sit in the dark on me own and not be bothered by the likes of you. Eh, look, it's your friend.

(The robin flutters around.)

MARY. Hello Mr Robin.

(The robin flies off.)

Where's he going?

BEN. He's got a life of his own, Lord only knows.

MARY. I'm going to follow him.

(She follows the robin off.)

BEN. You mind where you go. Hey! What have I told you, stick to the paths! *(Exits)*

(She chases after the robin, who loops around and lands behind her. She keeps turning round to see him and, each time she does, he flies over her head to land behind her again. They are both enjoying the game. It turns into grandmother's footsteps, whereby each time **MARY** *has her back to him, he hops towards her, then she whips round to catch him moving, and he freezes and starts pecking as if he's innocent.)*

Mary You! I was supposed to be following you, now you're following me!

(The robin tweets in response, then starts pecking the ground at one particular place.)

What are you doing? Digging for food?

(He carries on pecking then starts dancing around on the spot.)

What have you found?

(The robin pulls a worm out of the soil and brandishes it proudly, before depositing it on **MARY***'s lap.)*

Urgh!

(She throws it away. The robin cocks his head sarcastically at her then goes off to eat the worm on his own, at a distance.)

Oh. Sorry Mr Bird.

(The robin hops back over, then goes back to pecking at a new spot.)

What is that? What is it?

(She digs it up with her hands, and when she pulls it out, it's a key!)

A key! Is it the key to the secret garden? You knew, you knew all along!

(The robin twitters and bounces about, then flies off.)

Mr Robin!

Scene Nine

One Man and his Dog

(*Inside the house, later,* MRS MEDLOCK *and* MARTHA *catch* MARY *on her way past.*)

MRS MEDLOCK. Mary Lennox, how did you get in a state like that?

MARY. I fell in the wheelbarrow.

MRS MEDLOCK. You'll be dragging the mud in all over the house. And your hair! It's rough as a wild cat. Can't you try and look a little respectable.

MARY. Why do I need to look respectable to go to my room?

MRS MEDLOCK. You're not to go to your room. You're to meet your Uncle.

MARY. Uncle Craven! But –

MRS MEDLOCK. This way.

(MARY *looks at* MARTHA *fearfully. Scary music.* MRS MEDLOCK *leads the way.*)

MRS MEDLOCK. I hope you're on your best behaviour, for your Uncle never sees a soul, so you'd best be a good, quiet child.

(*They are standing outside a big door.*)

MR CRAVEN. (*Off*) Come!

(*They push the door and we are inside* MR CRAVEN*'s study. It is dark and gloomy and at the far end lurks a hunched figure. An enormous ugly grey dog is prowling.* MR CRAVEN *doesn't turn round.*)

MR CRAVEN. So this is her. The girl.

MRS MEDLOCK. Yes, Sir.

MR CRAVEN. Leave us.

MRS MEDLOCK. Would you like me to wait outside?

MR CRAVEN. I'd like you to go.

(The dog looks at her menacingly.)

MRS MEDLOCK. As you wish. *(Exits)*

*(***MARY*** stands silent, not knowing what to do. She takes a step forward, the grim dog growls. **MARY** jumps back.)*

MR CRAVEN. So. Well. Mary. *(Pause. He has prepared a speech but now doesn't know quite what to say).* I hope… I hope Misselthwaite is to your liking. It is a long while since young people roamed about here. I'm sure there are places which, had your parents not…if the circumstances had been different… Suffice to say, I hope you find it satisfactory. Well? Do you?

(She doesn't reply.)

Mary?

(The dog growls.)

MARY. Yes. *(Remembering)* Yes, Sir.

MR CRAVEN. And are you well?

MARY. Well? Yes, Sir.

MR CRAVEN. They take good care of you?

MARY. Yes, Sir.

MR CRAVEN. And are you lonely?

MARY. Lonely?

MR CRAVEN. Yes, solitary. As I am. Do you feel alone?

MARY. Sometimes.

MR CRAVEN. I am sorry for your loss.

MARY. I'm sorry for yours.

*(***MR CRAVEN*** is a little taken aback.)*

MR CRAVEN. Thank you. Thank you. *(Pause)* It's not easy, is it. I think we both know that.

MARY. *(Pause)* What's wrong with your back?

MR CRAVEN. I only wish I knew. It's unsightly, isn't it. Do I scare you?

MARY. A little. Have you always been – like that?

MR CRAVEN. Since I was a boy. There was a time when it troubled me less. When my wife was alive. But now, as you see, it is my lot. *(Pause)* What do you need, here. To fill your time. A nurse? A governess?

MARY. No, thank you. Dickon is teaching me things.

MR CRAVEN. But do you want for anything? Books? Paper? Is there anything you would like to help ease your way.

MARY. No. Except...

MR CRAVEN. Go on.

MARY. If I found a place...if I could find a patch of earth, just a small bit that no-one cared for, a place where I could make things grow...

MR CRAVEN. Grow?

MARY. I'd like to see it. Shoots growing out of the earth. If I could have some seeds to plant –

MR CRAVEN. *(Quietly)* That's enough.

MARY. But you said...if I could make some plants grow –

MR CRAVEN. *(Quietly)* Don't talk about it –

MARY. I'm sorry?

MR CRAVEN. *(Cross)* Don't talk like that! There's to be no talk of... I don't want to hear it, Mary.

(**MR CRAVEN** *has caught a closer look at her face and stands staring. She's terrified.*)

Good God. It's not possible! Come here.

(**MARY** *shakes her head.*)

Let me see your face. Come here.

MARY. You're scaring me –

(*He moves towards her.*)

MR CRAVEN. Your face...it can't be. It can't be! You need to go.

MARY. Sorry?

MR CRAVEN. Get out, get out of here! I can't look at you, please, please! Get out!

(The dog launches towards **MARY**, *and she runs for the door.* **MR CRAVEN** *howls and the dog barks and* **MARY** *wants to cry. She runs and runs down various corridors, getting lost, until she is bewildered. Then she sees the mouse.)*

MARY. You! How do I get back?

(The mouse squeaks and she follows it along the corridors until the mouse stops.)

But this isn't my room.

(All of a sudden there's a cry from somewhere nearby.)

It's coming from inside!

(The cry happens again. The mouse disappears under the door.)

Oh no, no!

(She says a very quick prayer.)

Dear Jesus, I'm sorry if I was ever bad, I'm sorry for all the naughty things I've done, especially for telling Raman that there was a crocodile in the sandpit when it was just my foot and for stealing his jelapi when he wasn't looking. I'm sorry, I'm sorry, amen. One – two –

(…and she pushes the door open.)

Scene Ten

Colin

(**MARY** *arrives in* **COLIN CRAVEN***'s bedroom. A boy with a face the colour of ivory is lying in a bed. He is wearing odd dark glasses and various mechanical accoutrements to keep him from moving. He is weak, and more sour than a crab apple.*)

COLIN. Who are you? Are you a ghost?

MARY. No. Are you?

COLIN. No. I'm Colin Craven.

MARY. And I'm Mary Lennox. What are you doing here?

COLIN. What do you mean, what am I doing here? What are you doing here? I've always been here.

MARY. What are all those metal things? Are you a prisoner? Or a criminal?

COLIN. Don't be stupid.

MARY. And why are you wearing sunglasses? Are you on holiday?

COLIN. Don't laugh at me!

MARY. I'm not.

COLIN. They're smoked glass. I have to wear them so the sunlight doesn't hurt my eyes. And these are my calipers. They keep me still because I'm sick. Really sick. And if I move, I might die. So don't touch me.

MARY. Why would I want to touch you?

COLIN. What are you doing here?

MARY. I live here. Mr Craven is my Uncle.

COLIN. Your Uncle? He's my father.

MARY. Your father? But…so you're my cousin. And you're here. Why did no-one say?

COLIN. The servants are forbidden from mentioning me. Father can't look at me. He only visits when I'm asleep. I don't think he likes me. I think maybe he hates me.

MARY. Why?

COLIN. I remind him of my mother. And she died and it broke his heart. So now he doesn't want to see me. That's why they shut me away. If I live they say I'll be a hunchback, like he is, and he can't bear it, but I shan't live.

MARY. How do you know?

COLIN. Everybody knows. Ever since I remember, people have said it. They used to think I was too young to understand. And now they think I don't hear, but I do.

MARY. But a doctor could help you.

COLIN. My doctor's my father's cousin. He's quite poor and if I die, he'll inherit Misselthwaite when father dies. I'm sure he'd be glad if I was dead. So would Mrs Medlock – and father, I'm sure – 'cause I only make them sad. I bet they'd all rather I'd just hurry up and die.

MARY. But don't you want to live?

COLIN. I don't know. Why would I? It's so lonely here. Sometimes, when I think of it, it makes me cry.

MARY. I heard you.

COLIN. No you didn't. I don't cry out loud.

MARY. It's alright to cry. I cried when I got here.

COLIN. But you're a girl.

MARY. So? We're just the same, it's just boys have dangly bits.

(He looks at her taken aback, then starts to laugh. She joins in.)

COLIN. Why did you come here?

MARY. My parents died, in India.

COLIN. You're Indian?

MARY. Don't be stupid, I'm not a native. I'm the daughter of the Viscount.

COLIN. Did you ever meet a fakir?

MARY. How do you know about fakirs?

COLIN. I've read about them in my books. I've read all four volumes of Magic and Enchantment, the Complete History of Sorcery. I'm an expert.

MARY. I bet you don't know everything.

COLIN. I bet I do. I know all about the mystic clock, and Mephistopheles' hat, and the Hindu cup trick.

MARY. But you've never seen it happen. In front of your eyes.

COLIN. Have you? You have, haven't you? You have to tell me.

MARY. I don't have to do anything.

COLIN. You do. You do if I want you to. I'm the Master of this house.

MARY. Your dad is.

(MARY *gets up to leave.*)

COLIN. Stop! Wait! You can't just leave!

MARY. So get up and stop me.

COLIN. I can't stand up! You know that, you're doing it on purpose.

MARY. Then stop being so utterly rotten and ask me nicely. "Mary, please will you tell me about the Indian cup trick?" Well?

(COLIN *is stubborn. Will he or won't he?*)

(*Cut to… In another part of the house,* MR CRAVEN *is looking for* MRS MEDLOCK.)

MR CRAVEN. Mrs Medlock? Mrs Medlock!

MRS MEDLOCK. Gracious, are you quite alright?

MR CRAVEN. I can't be here. I have to leave. I hadn't realised. The girl…

MRS MEDLOCK. Sir?

MR CRAVEN. She looks just like her.

MRS MEDLOCK. I should have thought to warn you. I can move her to the East Wing, you'll be sure not to run into her –

MR CRAVEN. No, don't punish her. It's not her doing. Listen, I've been talking to a doctor in Switzerland. She thinks she may be able to do something for my back.

MRS MEDLOCK. She?

MR CRAVEN. Yes, a Doctor Brés. She's something of a pioneer.

MRS MEDLOCK. Sir, I've never heard of a lady doctor before.

MR CRAVEN. Nor I, but she's French, so anything's possible. I shall go to London to make the arrangements on Monday.

MRS MEDLOCK. If you're sure, Sir.

MR CRAVEN. It's my only hope.

MRS MEDLOCK. In any case, it will do you good to get away. Mountain air, it might be curative. For more than just your back.

MR CRAVEN. You are right. You will look after Colin? And the girl.

MRS MEDLOCK. Of course. Sir.

Scene Eleven

The Secret Garden

(**MARY** *is skipping in the garden, following the robin.*)

MARY. Hey, slow down. Where are you going?

(*Music. The robin leads her on a long chase all round the grounds.*)

Stop, stop! You're too fast, I can't keep up.

(*She trips, landing on her knees.*)

Ow! I told you we were too quick.

(*As she looks up, she spots something in the wall along side her.*)

What's that?

(*Her expression changes to one of wonder.*)

It can't be. (*She looks closer*) A keyhole! Mr Robin, you knew!

(*She nervously takes the key from round her neck. Magical transformation as she steps into...the Secret Garden. As she watches, the garden grows around her. The plants seem to sing. It is a magical place. She walks around it, unable to believe her eyes.*)

It's like a jungle. It's like India.

(*Cut to* **MR CRAVEN** *visiting* **COLIN**, *who is asleep in bed.*)

MR CRAVEN. Sweet boy. Tomorrow I'm going away – to the mountains and the snow. Your mother would have liked it there; on the crags there are rock jasmine and lupines. They said the walking will be good for my back. Look at you. So peaceful. Sometimes I can hardly bear it.

(He kisses him and leaves.)

(Cut to a little while later, **MARTHA** *is walking across the lawn with her freshly gathered washing, when* **MARY** *catches her.)*

MARY. Martha, what are those white roots that look like onions?

MARTHA. You mean bulbs? The spring flowers grow from 'em. The small ones are snowdrops an' crocuses and the big ones are cyclamen and celandine.

MARY. But if they're white – if they're so pale they must have never seen the sun, are they dead? Can we save them?

MARTHA. I don't know. You'll have to ask Dickon. He can grow flowers out of a brick wall. *(She goes, then turns back to* **MARY***)* Why are you asking?

MARY. No reason. Thank you Martha!

*(***MARTHA*** exits.* **MARY** *turns we cut straight to mid conversation with* **DICKON***.)*

DICKON. Dead? No. They're only white cos they're fresh come up. Why do you ask? Mary?

MARY. I've found it.

DICKON. What?

MARY. I found the secret garden! But I think everything in it is dying, all shut in by itself with no-one to care for it. You need to help me make it live.

DICKON. Of course!

MARY. But you can't tell a soul.

DICKON. You know I wouldn't.

MARY. You have to promise. You have to say 'ghar ka bhedi lanka dhayey.'

DICKON. You made that up. That's just silly talk.

MARY. It's not. It's Hindi. It means he who holds the secret can destroy Lanka.

DICKON. What's lanka?

MARY. It's a city in Indian stories. A place where all the Rajahs rule. I think what it means is be careful who you tell secrets to. Here, take my hand.

DICKON. *(Taking her hand)* 'Gharka parka...

MARY. Dickon! You have to do it properly.

DICKON. *(Cheekily)* Sorry. *(He's not)*

(At that moment BEN arrives with his wheelbarrow, whistling as he goes.)

MARY. Quick! Hide!

(MARY and DICKON dive out of the way. BEN stops whistling and stands still. He's sure there's something funny going on.)

BEN. Eh? Must be me old age – I'd have sworn I saw some little weed or other.

(MARY and DICKON exchange glances.)

Hm. Maybe not.

(BEN continues on his way. MARY and DICKON re-emerge.)

MARY. That was close. We can't let anyone know. Ready?

DICKON. Ready.

MARY. 'Ghar ka bhedi lanka dhayey.'

DICKON. 'Ghar ka bhedi lanka dhayey.'

(They shake hands on it and as they do, we cut to them in the garden.)

DICKON. Well I never! Look at this place!

MARY. Is it dead? Are we too late?

DICKON. Is it dead? I've never seen owt more alive in me life! It's like nature's taken off her shoes and thrown herself down and rolled around and here it is – shoots and plants and life!

MARY. But look at all the dead wood.

DICKON. It's just nature playing a magic trick. Look here.

(He takes a knife out of his pocket and cuts into a piece of wood and reveals green inside.)

It's green inside. It's as wick as you or me. If we cut the old wood off and make some space for it, there'll be a fountain of roses by the time we're done. Though I'd bet there's been someone in here more recent than ten years hence.

MARY. There can't have been. The door was locked and the key was buried.

DICKON. Someone's pruned it, I'd swear to it.

(Cut to MRS MEDLOCK and MARTHA in a corridor. They are removing their face masks, after visiting COLIN.)

MRS MEDLOCK. You heard the doctor, we have to keep him still.

MARTHA. He had a cramp. And he looks so sad! I hate it when he cries.

MRS MEDLOCK. I know. And if there was any other way... but Dr Craven knows best. We must put our faith in him. And in Jesus.

MARTHA. Jesus doesn't have to listen to him yowling through the night.

MRS MEDLOCK. You watch your mouth. We must do as we are told, for Colin's sake, and his Father's.

MARTHA. I think Mr Craven is dying.

MRS MEDLOCK. Why on earth would you say a wicked thing like that?

MARTHA. His hunch is getting worse.

MRS MEDLOCK. They're going to try and heal him. In Switzerland.

MARTHA. In Switzerland?! Do you think he might like a maid to go with him?

MRS MEDLOCK. Now that really would be the death of him. Be off with you.

(Cut to COLIN and MARY.)

COLIN. I wanted to draw you but now it's too late.

MARY. Why would you want to draw me?

COLIN. Because I'm an artist. I'm very talented.

MARY. Would you make me look ugly on purpose?

COLIN. No...not on purpose.

MARY. Colin!

COLIN. Can I draw you tomorrow?

MARY. No. I don't like sitting still.

COLIN. Well what do you like?

MARY. Crumble. And tea cake. And playing outside with Dickon.

COLIN. Who's Dickon?

MARY. He's my friend.

COLIN. Why do you need another friend? You have me.

MARY. I can have more than one. Dickon lives on the scarp.

COLIN. If I live, this land will all belong to me. But I don't suppose I will. I'll probably die soon.

MARY. Don't be stupid. You're only ten.

COLIN. How do you know I'm ten?

MARY. Because ten years ago they locked the garden door.

COLIN. What garden door? *(Pause)* What garden door?

MARY. You mustn't tell anyone.

COLIN. Who would I tell? You're the only one that talks to me.

MARY. There's a garden. It was your mother's, and it's the most precious place in the world. But when she died, Mr Craven locked it up and no-one's found it since.

COLIN. You mean it's a secret garden?

MARY. Yes.

COLIN. Someone must have been in.

MARY. They haven't.

COLIN. Well ask the gardeners!

MARY. They won't talk about it.

COLIN. I'll make them.

MARY. No!

COLIN. But I want to see it!

MARY. But then it'll never be secret again.

COLIN. What?

MARY. Don't you see? If no-one knew but us, if we could find the hidden door, and shut it behind us we could call it our garden, and pretend that – that we're mistlethrushes, and that it's our nest – and we could make it come alive!

COLIN. Is it dead?

MARY. It will be if no-one cares for it. It was all overgrown and tangled when we found it, but now we've cut the dead away… Oops.

COLIN. You've found it!

MARY. Please don't tell. We have to save it. Promise or I'll never come and see you again. Promise, Colin!

COLIN. I suppose. Though I'll never be able to sleep, now you've made me all excited.

MARY. When I couldn't sleep, Ayah would sing to me. I can sing to you if you like. You have to close your eyes, and think of what you want to dream about –

COLIN. The Secret Garden.

MARY. That's a good dream. Now think of the wrens and the skylarks, and the fox in the night time, and the owls watching out from their nests.

(*MARY begins to sing. As she does* **COLIN** *drifts off to sleep.*)

SONG 2: CHANDA MAAMA DOOR KE

CHANDAA MAAMA DOOR KE, PUYE PAKAAYEN BOOR KE,
CHANDAA MAAMA DOOR KE, PUYE PAKAAYEN BOOR KE,
AAP KHAAYEN THAALI MEIN, MUNNE KO DEN PYAALI MEIN.

(*REPEAT AS DESIRED*)

(*Simultaneously,* **DICKON** *appears in the garden and continues gardening, with the help of the animals, who sing too.*)

(Simultaneously, on another part of the stage – Lord Craven arrives in the servants quarters with his dog and two large bags.)

MR CRAVEN. Mrs Medlock.

MRS MEDLOCK. Sir?

MR CRAVEN. I want you to burn these.

MRS MEDLOCK. But Sir... *(Looking in the bags)* Her gowns?

MR CRAVEN. Clear them out of the house. Or give them away, I don't know. Just get them out of here.

MRS MEDLOCK. But Sir –

MR CRAVEN. You must do it while I'm away.

MRS MEDLOCK. If you change your / mind?

MR CRAVEN. I've lived like this for too long. It is time.

*(He leaves the bags marches onwards. **MRS MEDLOCK** stands, bewildered. The song builds to a crescendo.)*

(Interval)

ACT TWO

Scene One

Treatment

(**COLIN** *is lying in his invalid chair.* **MARY** *has just arrived.* **COLIN** *is furious with her.*)

COLIN. You said you'd come this morning.

MARY. I said I'd come today, I didn't say when.

COLIN. I've been on my own all day.

MARY. Don't be sour. I've been in the garden with Dickon.

COLIN. You're always with Dickon.

MARY. That's because he's kind and gentle and he does magic with animals.

COLIN. Well I hate him.

MARY. That is a shame.

COLIN. Why?

(**DICKON** *enters.*)

DICKON. Hello, Colin.

MARY. Colin, meet Dickon.

COLIN. What are you doing here?

DICKON. I came to see thee.

COLIN. But you're from the outside; you'll bring germs in and make me ill! Go away, go away!

MARY. Dickon won't make you ill, that's ridiculous.

COLIN. Out there there are spores that'll fill my lungs and make me choke – they'll be on his clothes.

DICKON. No more than on hers.

COLIN. But you're a cottager, the moor's full of disease.

DICKON. Eh, it's not the moor that'll make thee ill. It's being shut up indoors. Nowt can grow in the dark.

COLIN. The doctor said the spores would infect me and the light would blind me and that going outside would kill me for sure. You wouldn't understand.

(DICKON *is unwrapping a small bundle.*)

What's that?

DICKON. I'll show you if you mend your manners.

(DICKON *unwraps a newborn lamb from inside the blankets.*)

COLIN. Oh! Oh!

DICKON. He's a newborn, only few days old so he don't yet know how to stand. Would you like to hold him?

COLIN. I don't know how.

DICKON. Keep him wrapped. Cradle him like tha would a babe. Here. He's fragile, for he's lost his Mother.

(*He hands him over.* COLIN *is entranced.*)

COLIN. Who'll take care of him?

DICKON. I'll have to be Ma to 'im. I mightn't look much like her, but I'll feed him and help him stand. Then, when he's strong I'll show him t'other creatures on the moor and they can be his family.

COLIN. He licked my hand!

DICKON. He thinks tha hand's a teat! He likes thee.

(*There's a commotion outside.*)

MARY. Who's that?!

COLIN. It's Medlock and the Doctor. They're here for my treatment. They mustn't catch you here.

MARY. We have to hide.

DICKON. Where?

COLIN. They're coming!

MARY. Quick – behind here!

(DICKON *and* MARY *dive out of sight. A beat, then* COLIN *realises he's still holding the lamb, and covers it up with his bedclothes, tucking it out of sight just as* MRS MEDLOCK *enters with* DR CRAVEN *and* MARTHA *(and possibly other staff).* MRS MEDLOCK *is holding a shiny metal tray with some medical paraphernalia on it. All are wearing linen facemasks to cover their mouths.)*

DR CRAVEN. Afternoon, boy.

MRS MEDLOCK. Good gracious, why are your blankets loose?

DR CRAVEN. Did you loosen them?

MRS MEDLOCK. Of course not. I only do as you instruct.

DR CRAVEN. I've told you before – he must stay covered up at all times. You must do better.

MRS MEDLOCK. I've kept him still, and quiet and in the dark as you told me!

DR CRAVEN. Something's different about him. Master Colin, you are quite sure you're alright?

COLIN. I'm perfectly alright.

DR CRAVEN. You haven't been getting excited have you? You know excitement is dangerous for weaklings.

COLIN. No Sir.

DR CRAVEN. Good, good. Skin is pale, hair is thin. No signs of improvement at all. You are a sickly child, Colin. Let us commence your exercises.

COLIN. No, please!

MRS MEDLOCK. You mustn't be ungrateful. You're such a lucky child, to have a doctor make you a special machine to fix your bones. No other child's got that.

COLIN. They can have it.

MRS MEDLOCK. Master Colin!

DR CRAVEN. Without it your muscles will waste away and you will die.

COLIN. But I hate being stretched!

MRS MEDLOCK. We will try to be gentle.

DR CRAVEN. Mrs Medlock! We are not in the business of patting and stroking – if he's to survive he must bear the pain. Now, put him into position.

(Just at this moment COLIN *takes the opportunity to pass the lamb in the bundle to* DICKON, *who out momentarily before disappearing again in the nick of time.)*

MARTHA. Dickon!

MRS MEDLOCK. What did you say?

MARTHA. I said… I said…

*(*MARTHA *spies* MARY *in her hiding place.* MARY *puts her finger to her mouth to silence* MARTHA.)*

I said Di…dn't you want me to help thee?

MRS MEDLOCK. That's exactly what I said. What's wrong with you, foolish girl?

DR CRAVEN. Ready to begin?

COLIN. Please, please don't use the electricals! I'm stretched enough already.

DR CRAVEN. Don't you want to get better?

*(*DR CRAVEN *and* MRS MEDLOCK *fix electrical nodes to* COLIN's *legs. When they turn the machine on, it forces his legs to shoot forwards, thereby stretching them out.)*

DR CRAVEN. Three, two, one!

COLIN. Ow!

DR CRAVEN. And again, three, two, one!

COLIN. Argh! Stop, stop!

DR CRAVEN. One more round, turn it up.

COLIN. But I'm all stretched.

MRS MEDLOCK. Listen to the doctor, Colin.

DR CRAVEN. One more round, I say!

(From under the bed there's a baaing sound.)

What was that?

(There's another baa.)

It sounds like –

MARTHA. It was me! It's the electricals – it made me go funny. Look, do it again.

(*The Doctor presses the button and* MARTHA *presents to vibrate and makes a 'baa' sound. He tries it again, she does it again.*)

Baaa! See. I can't help it, tis the vibrations.

MRS MEDLOCK. Maybe it's Martha you should be treating. I think her brain's gone soft.

DR CRAVEN. That will do for today. Tomorrow we'll double the dosage.

COLIN. No. I'll scream even louder.

MRS MEDLOCK. Master Colin, we are only trying to make you better. And what about his supper, Sir?

DR CRAVEN. Only feed him a little, a quarter portion at most. And nothing rich, in case it disturbs his digestion. I prescribe a light water-based broth with a little salt and lemon juice. No meat, no starch and definitely no fruit or vegetables.

MRS MEDLOCK. Are you sure?

DR CRAVEN. Fruit and vegetables would be a terrible mistake.

MRS MEDLOCK. As you wish, Sir.

DR CRAVEN. Master Colin, until tomorrow.

MRS MEDLOCK. Martha, you turn down the bed while I fetch the broth.

COLIN. Is my father going to visit?

MRS MEDLOCK. I'm afraid not. He's gone to Switzerland, to improve his spine. He shan't be back for several months.

COLIN. Why can't I go to Switzerland to make me better?

DR CRAVEN. Master Colin, you are gravely ill. You are weak, your body does not support you. Your body does not like you. Any disturbance and it might reject you completely and leave you like a shriveled shell. You are not going anywhere. Mrs Medlock, you must keep him tied down and out of the light. It is the only path to recovery.

MRS MEDLOCK. Yes, Sir. Let me show you out.

(They both leave. A beat.)

MARY. What were they doing to you?

MARTHA. You two! What are you doing here? And where are your masks? You'll make him ill.

MARY. We won't. It's all lies! You can't get better being tied down like that.

MARTHA. If Mrs Medlock finds you here, she'll have my guts and she'll have thee sent away. She's afeared he'll die and she'll get the blame.

COLIN. I am here, you know!

MARTHA. Sorry.

(DICKON investigates the machine and accidentally gives himself a shock.)

DICKON. Ow! What is this?

COLIN. It's the stretching machine. It sends electricals in me, like spikes that make me feel like my bones are exploding. But it keeps me alive.

DICKON. Keeps thee alive, giving thee jolts like that?! What would keep thee alive is stretching tha legs in the grass and standing upon them as they're meant for.

COLIN. But I'm too weak.

MARTHA. And the doctor said it makes him better.

MARY. What if the doctor doesn't want to make him better?! Colin, you said that if you die, the doctor will inherit the house.

MARTHA. Master Colin, is that true?!

MARY. What if he's trying to kill you?!

COLIN. He's not trying to kill me – he's a doctor!

MARY. But you said he didn't want you to live.

COLIN. No-one wants to me to live. Everyone says I'll die.

MARY. If everyone said I was dying I'd stay alive on purpose just to spite them. We need to set him free, get him out of his binds.

COLIN. What? No!

(MARY *pulls* COLIN*'s glasses off and he screws up his eyes.*)

Hey, give them back! I'm blind! Argh, the light!

MARY. Take off the calipers. Quickly!

MARTHA. But Mrs Medlock!

(DICKON *tries to remove the calipers.*)

COLIN. What are you doing? Get off me!

(*He smacks* DICKON *who reels away.*)

DICKON. Ow!

MARY. He was trying to set you free! You're the most rotten, selfish, callous boy I've ever met.

COLIN. I don't care! Go away!

MARY. Make me. Come on – get up and make me! You can't order me around like I'm your Ayah.

COLIN. I'm the Master of this house and you have to do as I say.

(*As he speaks,* COLIN *angrily thrusts himself forward and realises his calipers are off, and he is free of them.*)

MARY. Colin, you're free!

(COLIN *realises there's nothing holding him down. A beat while he decides whether this is a good thing or not. Then he has an almighty unstoppable tantrum –*)

COLIN. Aargh, I'm going to die!

MARY. What do you know about dying?

COLIN. My mother died!

MARY. So did mine, and I don't lie around crying about it all the time.

COLIN. And if I live I'll be a hunchback!

MARY. You won't.

COLIN. I will. I have a lump already. I can feel it!

MARY. *(To* **DICKON** *and* **MARTHA***)* Turn him over.

COLIN. No, no!

MARY. There's no lump, I'll prove it.

*(**MARTHA** and **DICKON** hold **COLIN** down while* **MARY** *climbs on top of him and feel his back.* **COLIN** *screams and cries. Suddenly* **MRS MEDLOCK** *arrives.* **MARY** *is caught in the act.)*

MRS MEDLOCK. What are you doing you wicked, wicked child!

MARY. He's not ill, the doctor is killing him!

MRS MEDLOCK. Get out of here, you little witch. What have you done, you'll kill him!

DICKON. We's helping him.

MRS MEDLOCK. *(To* **MARTHA***)* You! You let that wretched girl in here. That's it, one too many times, get out. You're finished here.

MARTHA. But Ma'am!

MRS MEDLOCK. Get out of here and pack your bags.

(Meanwhile **COLIN** *has caught sight of himself in the metal tray which* **MRS MEDLOCK** *left, and now holds it, staring at his reflection in it.)*

MARTHA. Please / Ma'am!

COLIN. Stop, stop! Look at my face.

(During the commotion, no-one had noticed that **COLIN** *had managed to turn himself over and sit up.)*

MRS MEDLOCK. Bless me!

MARTHA. You've turned yourself over!

DICKON. And sat yourself up!

COLIN. But look at my face. It's not white like bone. It's pink. Pink like healthy skin. Mary – you did this.

MRS MEDLOCK. Master Colin –

COLIN. Be quiet, Mrs Medlock. Mary! When you looked at my back...was there a lump? Please. Tell me the truth.

(They all look at MARY.*)*

MRS MEDLOCK. Well, was there?

MARY. No. There was nothing.

COLIN. No lump? Nothing at all?

MARY. Nothing at all.

MRS MEDLOCK. You don't know what you're talking about.

MARY. It's just bones that stick out 'cause the Doctor won't let you eat.

MRS MEDLOCK. Mary!

COLIN. So I won't be a hunchback?

MARY. No, Colin, you won't.

MRS MEDLOCK. Young lady, don't you dare go giving a sickly boy false hopes. That is a wicked thing to do. The doctor knows what's best and you've no place –

COLIN. Mrs Medlock, if you try and send Martha away, I will scream so loud that I'll wake up the whole house. Martha is an excellent nurse. She is not to leave, I forbid it. But I want you to go.

MRS MEDLOCK. Me? But Sir!

COLIN. You're to go back to the kitchen, and leave me with my friends. That's my order.

MRS MEDLOCK. But your health, Master Colin...

COLIN. I can feel a fit coming on. I'm getting hot, I'm getting shaky, if you don't go now, you'll be sorry!

(He starts pretending to fit.)

MRS MEDLOCK. Alright, alright – I've gone, if only to keep you from doing yourself an injury.

(And she's gone. COLIN *stops immediately.)*

COLIN. You can go too Martha.

MARTHA. Yes, Sir. Sir? Did you mean that, what you said about me being an excellent nurse?

COLIN. I suppose I did.

MARTHA. Oh. Right. Only I think that's the first nice thing you've ever said to me. Eh, I never thought you like me. He likes me! Do you really me or do you really, really / like me?

COLIN. *(Quickly)* Go away, Martha.

MARTHA. Yes Sir.

(And she's gone.)

COLIN. How much of it is lies?

MARY. I don't know.

COLIN. Do you think it's possible that I'm not ill?

DICKON. Sir, last spring I found a fox cub that was so thin and spindly, I thought he'd never survive. But I took him on t' moor and met him with the hare and the badger pup, and every day he got a bit stronger. He just wanted for company, and fresh air. And now he capers all about, like nowt was ever wrong with 'im. You could do it.

COLIN. Do you think, if I practice sitting up, one day I might go outside and see the moor? Might I see the Secret Garden?

MARY. *(Indicating the lamb)* What does he think?

LAMB. Baaaa!

Scene Two

An Announcement

(The staff are assembled to listen to an announcement. **COLIN** *appears in his wicker wheelchair, pushed by* **MARY** *and* **DICKON**. *He has the lamb in a bundle on his knee.)*

MRS PHIPPS. Blow me down, it's never Master Colin! What's happened to him? Did you know about this?

MARTHA. Definitely not.

MRS PHIPPS. Bless my soul, there's colour in his face.

COLIN. I have called you all together to make a very important announcement. This morning I will be going outside.

(There is a stir around the group.)

I am to go out in my chair into the gardens and I will be accompanied by Miss Mary and Master Dickon. I may be back for luncheon. I may be back for tea. I may go out every day if I choose.

MRS MEDLOCK. Maybe not every day –

COLIN. And when I am outside, none of you are to follow me. No-one. I must be left to do as I please. Most importantly of all, none of you are to breathe a word to my father. He is not to know. Is that clear?

(Mutters of concern pass between the staff.)

You know the rules! When Father is absent, I am Master of the house, and I say he is not to know. That is all. You may go.

(They all go. **MRS MEDLOCK** *approaches to steer the wheelchair.)*

MRS MEDLOCK. Right then.

COLIN. What are you doing?

MRS MEDLOCK. What do you mean? I am taking you outside, as you insist.

COLIN. No, you're not. You're to stay here, in the house.

MRS MEDLOCK. But Master Colin –

COLIN. I am the Master of the house and I say you're to stay inside. *(To* MARY *and* DICKON*)* Come on!

(They go off triumphantly. MRS MEDLOCK *looks terribly hurt. She notices* MARTHA *is hanging around.)*

MRS MEDLOCK. What are you looking at? Haven't you got socks to wash?

(They leave, though MRS MEDLOCK *can't help watching him go with concern.)*

Scene Three

First Steps

(**MARY** *and* **DICKON** *are pushing* **COLIN** *through the grounds.*)

COLIN. Come on, let's go faster. Faster! Faster!

(*Music. The three of them race around getting quicker and quicker until they're outside the Secret Garden.*)

MARY. Are you ready?

COLIN. I can't wait.

DICKON. I think tha should close tha eyes.

MARY. Then it'll be a proper surprise.

COLIN. What do you think, Bud?

MARY. Bud?

COLIN. Yes. I named him Bud because he came with the spring. Like a little sprout!

MARY. Bud. I think he likes it.

BUD. Baa.

DICKON. I told thee, tha'd a friend for life in him.

MARY. Close your eyes, then. And you, Bud.

(**COLIN** *closes his eyes and Bud tucks his head under* **COLIN**'s *blanket so that he can be surprised too.* **MARY** *and* **DICKON** *push* **COLIN** *into the Secret Garden.*)

MARY. You can open them now.

(**COLIN** *very slowly opens his eyes. Bud looks out from under the blanket and baas with delight.* **COLIN** *can't believe the vision in front of him, a haven of growth and* *spring. The garden springs to life and seems to fill the air with music.)*

(As the music plays, MARY *and* DICKON *wheel* COLIN *round the garden, showing him their work.* COLIN *is delighted.)*

COLIN. It's like magic. Like pictures in books.

MARY. It's glorious.

COLIN. No wonder mother loved it here.

DICKON. And your father.

COLIN. I dreamt he came to see me, before he went away. I dreamt it, but I don't know if it was real.

MARY. What happened, in the dream?

COLIN. He was afraid to look at me. I think his heart might actually be broken, like a glass animal that can't be mended. I think he doesn't want to love me, in case I die like mother did.

MARY. Then you'll just have to stay alive. Look at you. The pale's already begun to creep away.

DICKON. You're like a winter root, we just need to thaw you out and water you and make you grow. Like Bud. Look, he's almost up on his hinds.

(Bud is trying to stand up.)

MARY. He's trying to stand. He's learning to stand up!

(They watch the lamb. Slowly Bud manages to stand on four wobbly legs and take a step or too before overbalancing and collapsing back onto the rug. They all cheer – and as they do a head appears over the fence. It is BEN WEATHERSTAFF *and he has a grim expression on his face. He hasn't seen* COLIN, *as* MARY *is in front of him.)*

BEN. You! What are you doing in here! You know it's not allowed, you meddlesome wench!

MARY. But we've been making the garden grow.

BEN. What're you trying to do, lose me my job? You knows no-one's allowed inside. Get out – get thee out of there –

MARY. But the garden was dying!

BEN. Don't make me get me pitch fork out –

(Just then a voice comes from behind **MARY***.)*

COLIN. You most certainly will not get your pitch fork out.

BEN. What? Who are – oh Lord.

*(***MARY*** moves out of the way and* **BEN** *sees* **COLIN** *sitting on the blanket.)*

COLIN. Don't you talk to my friend like that. Do you know who I am?

BEN. You're… Sir, you're Master Craven, the little cripple.

COLIN. I'm not a little cripple.

BEN. You're the hunchback.

MARY. He's not.

COLIN. I'm not a hunchback!

BEN. But you've got a crooked back.

COLIN. Who said I have a crooked back?

BEN. And crooked legs.

COLIN. I haven't. I haven't!! I'm not sick and I'm not a hunchback and I don't have crooked legs – I'll prove it!

(He tries to launch himself to his feet defiantly but he falls, crumpled.)

MARY. Colin!

(For a moment we think he's injured. But **COLIN** *won't give up. He is determined.)*

COLIN. Mary, take my hand.

MARY. But –

COLIN. Take it. And you, Dickon.

(*MARY and* DICKON *both take one of* COLIN*'s hands.*
And then very slowly, struggling with every movement,
COLIN *attempts to get to his feet.*)

MARY. Come on. Come on. You can do it. You can do it.

COLIN. It hurts.

MARY. You can do it, / you can do it!

DICKON. You can do it!

MARY. You can do it, you are doing it!

COLIN. I'm standing, I'm standing up!

DICKON. He's standing up!

BEN. Sweet Lord Jesus in Heaven.

COLIN. Mary, stand there.

(*He indicates a few paces away.* MARY *does as he says.*
DICKON *supports* COLIN *who, very slowly, takes one*
step, then another.)

BEN. Blow me down.

COLIN. Take your hands away.

DICKON. Are you sure?

COLIN. I'm sure. Ready?

(DICKON *releases his hold and* COLIN *stands on his*
own, wobbly at first until he finds his balance. Very,
slowly COLIN *takes his first solo step. Then another,*
then another, until he reaches MARY *and collapses into*
her arms. DICKON *then joins in and the three of them*
embrace with joy. Bud, who has now got almost full use
of his legs, bounces at their feet and tries to join in.)

BEN. Well, I never! Blessed be the day.

(*Jubilation.*)

Scene Four

Diagnosis

(In Switzerland, **DOCTOR MADELEINE BRÉS** *holds a sheaf of x-rays.* **MR CRAVEN** *waits nervously.)*

MR CRAVEN. So, Doctor?

DR BRÉS. Well. You are certainly an unusual case. Your spine is twisted, severely, and I am afraid, without care, the hunch that so concerns you will only become more pronounced. In the worst case, you may no longer be able to walk.

MR CRAVEN. Well… Right.

DR BRÉS. But – there is good news. There is hope, je pense.

MR CRAVEN. How so?

DR BRÉS. Mr Craven, when I looked at your x-rays I ran every test I know to find the bone defect, the skeletal abnormality which has, in recent years, made your condition worse.

MR CRAVEN. And what did you find?

DR BRÉS. Rien. Nothing. Nothing at all.

MR CRAVEN. I don't understand.

DR BRÉS. Mr Craven, there has always been a bend in your spine, but there is nothing wrong with your bones. Your skeleton is as it always has been. Your hunch is an acute case of muscular atrophy. The grief, the torment you have suffered has quite literally bent you, crushed you under its weight and forced your body to contort into this miserable state.

MR CRAVEN. You mean I've done this to myself?

DR BRÉS. Circumstances are responsible, not you. You are not to blame. But I am convinced that together we might at least improve you. It will take time and patience – and hard work – but I believe it is possible.

MR CRAVEN. Thank you, Doctor Brés. You are a remarkable woman.

DR BRÉS. I am a remarkable Doctor, Sir. The rest, you will understand, is simply anatomy.

(A frisson of tension... or is it chemistry?)

Scene Five

The Quest

(The children and **BEN** *are in the garden.)*

COLIN. What do you think he will say, when he sees me standing?

DICKON. And walking!

BEN. He'd be right proud of you, son. And so would your mother.

COLIN. Did you know my mother?

BEN. Did I know her? Aye, I knew her all right. I like to think she had a soft spot for old Ben. She'd allus bring me a biscuit when she came down from the house, and no other soul but me was allowed to tend to her roses. They were her very favourites, see. So when the garden was shut up – sometimes I came back, to tend to 'em.

DICKON. I said someone had been in!

MARY. But how did you get in? The key was buried and the door was locked.

BEN. Eh, I'm a Yorkshire man born and bred. And there ain't no proper fellah in Yorkshire who don't own a step ladder. I came in over the wall, didn't I! If only she could see thee now.

COLIN. I can't wait to show Father. But he won't be home for weeks.

MARY. Then we must bring him back.

COLIN. How?

DICKON. You could write to him.

COLIN. But we don't know where he is.

MARY. We could go on a quest to find him – in Switzerland!

DICKON. What, across the sea?!

COLIN. What'd we do, swim there?

MARY. Dickon could charm a whale to take us on its back. Mr Weatherstaff could sit up the front.

BEN. I'm quite happy here on the dry earth, thank you.

COLIN. I have an idea. But you have to listen to it properly and not laugh.

BEN. Yes, Sir!

COLIN. I always thought, if I was to live, I'd like to be a scientist and make discoveries.

MARY. What sort of discoveries?

COLIN. Discoveries about magic. Scarcely anyone knows anything about it, except people in old books. And Mary, a little, because she was born in India.

MARY. And Dickon, he's an animal charmer.

COLIN. *(Sharply)* Yes, I know, thank you! You see, I think there might be magic in everything, only we haven't sense enough to get hold of it and make it do things for us, like horses and electricity and steam. And it's everywhere, we just don't know what to call it. The magic in this garden helped me stand up. When I tried to stand, Mary kept saying "you can do it, you can do it", over and over again. And I did. I had to try too, but her magic helped me do it.

MARY. That's what fakir's do. One came to my father's party and he made himself float in the air. I walked right underneath him to see if there was anything holding him up, but there wasn't! And then, he threw a rope up in the air and made it stand up straight like a pole and then he climbed up it and disappeared! And all the time, he was chanting. The same words again and again.

COLIN. You see. When you say something over and over and think about it until it fills you up, you can make it real. I think we should do magic to get my Father to come home. I can chant.

DICKON. And I can play.

MARY. And I can sing an Indian charm.

COLIN. And what will you do, Mr Weatherstaff?

BEN. I don't believe in magic. Tis ungodly. I'm a church man.

COLIN. But God is the most magic thing of all.

DICKON. Maybe you could say a prayer, or sing a hymn?

BEN. I'll think about it.

MARY. We must do it tonight, when it's dark. Magic always happens in the dark.

DICKON. And we must do it here. For nature's full of magic.

COLIN. And we must stand in a circle and put something of Father's in the middle, to catch his spirit.

BEN. His old coat is in the outhouse, I could fetch that.

MARY. It needs to be something dear to him. Something important.

COLIN. The painting. There's a painting of mother.

DICKON. Where is it?

MARY. I've seen it. He hangs it in his study.

COLIN. Mary, you'll have to fetch it.

MARY. From his study?! Not a chance! That's where the dog is.

COLIN. It's the only way.

MARY. It only didn't eat me last time 'cause he stopped it. I can't!

COLIN. Mary. Please. *(Pause)* Please.

(A beat. MARY gives in. As she leaves, we see MR CRAVEN walking with DR BRÉS.)

DR BRÉS. You are doing well. Just breathe. The air is curative, non?

MR CRAVEN. I can feel it. Though my back is so stiff.

DR BRÉS. Perseverance, Monsieur.

MR CRAVEN. Archibald. Please.

DR BRÉS. Keep yourself moving. You must be limber, supple. You have already made remarkable progress.

MR CRAVEN. Where are we going?

DR BRÉS. There. To the top.

MR CRAVEN. To the summit?

DR BRÉS. If we begin now we should make it by midnight. Allez.

MR CRAVEN. But it'll be dark.

DR BRÉS. The stars will be our guide. And it is a full moon. On y va!

(And off they go, up the mountain.)

Scene Six

Taming the Beast

(**MARY** *and Mr Wildeebeast are journeying through the corridors to the study, hiding when* **MRS MEDLOCK** *passes. When they go inside, the grim dog is asleep in the middle of the floor, between them and the desk.* **MARY** *has to negotiate past him without waking him up. Every time she gets near, he stirs. Then suddenly he's on his feet and growling.*)

MARY. Oh no, no! Good dog, shhh! Mr Wildeebeast, help!

(*The mouse squeaks.*)

What?

(*The mouse squeaks again.*)

What are you saying?

(*The mouse squeaks again.*)

Squeaking won't help! Oh, wait...

(*She realises what the mouse is telling her.*)

Talk soft and sing gentle when you're speaking with nature.

(*She begins to sing* **DICKON**'s *song* (**Song of the Moor**) *to the dog. At first he growls, then as she gently moves towards him, soothing him, she lulls him into a woozy state. As he is listening to her, she indicates to the mouse to keep the dog occupied. The mouse performs a hypnotic sleepy dance as* **MARY** *sneaks round him and retrieves the portrait.*)

72

SONG OF THE MOOR: DOG LULLABY

TONGUE TIED IS THE SKY LARK
BUT HIS SONG, TIED TO THE BRIGHT ARC
OF THE WIND,
WHISTLES PAST THE BRISTLE CUP
AND THISTLES, UP AND DOWN.

QUIETENED IS THE HOUND NOW,
AS YOUR EYES CLOSE AND YOUR BROW BOWS,
INTO SLEEP,
GENTLE AS A LULLABY,
NO SECRETS SHALL YOU KEEP.

(The dog dozes off in a stupor and **MARY** *makes a run for it.)*

Good work, Mr Wildeebeast! I didn't know you could dance!

(Mr Wildeebeast squeaks with pride. Outside, in the corridor, **MARY** *bumps into* **MARTHA**, *and tries to hide the massive painting behind her back.)*

MARTHA. Mary! What are you doing? You know you're not allowed in this wing. *(Seeing the painting)* What's that?

MARY. Nothing.

MARTHA. It's the master's painting! Mary Lennox!

MARY. Shh!

MARTHA. What in heaven's name –

MARY. We need it. For a spell.

MARTHA. A spell?

MARY. Martha, if I tell you a very, very big secret – do you promise not to tell. *(Pause –* **MARTHA** *doesn't know if she can)* You have to promise not to tell a soul, or I can't take you with me.

MARTHA. Take me? Where?

MARY. You have to swear on your life.

MARTHA. I swear.

MARY. Come on then.

MARTHA. Where are we going?

MARY. To the Secret Garden!

Scene Seven

Magic

(Night time. **BEN, COLIN** *(on crutches) and* **DICKON** *are putting the final touches to the totem pole, which they've fashioned out of sticks, lanterns and garden paraphernalia.* **MARY** *arrives with the painting.)*

MARY. I've got it.

DICKON. You did it!

COLIN. Hang it here, on the totem pole.

MARY. Hey, that's good!

COLIN. Mr Weatherstaff helped us make it.

MARY. It's magnificent.

BEN. Eh, you'll make me blush.

*(***MARY*** hangs the painting on the pole. They stand back and admire their work.)*

DICKON. I think we're ready.

MARY. Not quite. I brought something else too. A special charm.

DICKON. What's that then?

*(***MARTHA*** emerges from the bushes.)*

BEN. Eh, you can't go bringing everyone in here.

MARY. She's not everyone, she's Martha. And she's my friend.

MARTHA. Master Colin, you're standing up.

COLIN. Not only that. Look at my legs! *(He shows her some moves)*

MARTHA. It's magic!

MARY. It is magic.

(A clock starts to strike twelve.)

COLIN. It's time. We have to do it now, while it's the witching hour.

MARY. *(To* **MARTHA***)* Do you know what to do?

MARTHA. I'm from the moor. We know all about magic on the moor.

*(*DICKON *begins to play his pipe.* MARY *begins singing her Indian song, then the other join in. They dance around the pole and evoke the spirit of* MR CRAVEN*.)*

SONG 3: CHANT

CHANDAA MAAMA DOOR KE, PUYE PAKAAYEN BOOR KE,

AAP KHAAYEN THAALI MEIN, MUNNE KO DEN PYAALI MEIN.

SEND OUR SONG ON RAVEN WING, SPIRIT OF THE RAVEN
    KING,

CATCH A SPIRIT IN THE RING, TO THE MOOR A CRAVEN
    BRING.

OVER DALE AND OVER SCARP, NIGHT OWL HOWL TO
    MOORISH HARP,

'CROSS THE OCEAN, PIPE OUR SONG AS DAY IS SHORT AND
    NIGHT IS LONG.

(As the song builds, we see MR CRAVEN *nearing the peak of the mountain with* DR BRÉS*.)*

DR BRÉS. Mon Dieu! Never have I seen the stars as clear as this.

(All of a sudden, he stops. A strange thing happens, the oddest feeling comes over him. She notices.)

Monsieur, you alright?

MR CRAVEN. I'm sorry, I feel...

DR BRÉS. You unwell? You look pale. The air here is thin –

MR CRAVEN. I'm not ill. I just... I have to get back.

DR BRÉS. Back? To the lodge?

MR CRAVEN. To England.

DR BRÉS. England? But we're almost at the summit! You can see it.

MR CRAVEN. I'm sorry. I can't explain it. I just have to go. Thank you – really. You have done me more good than you'll ever know. *(He starts to leave, shouting back as he goes)* I will write to you! Thank you – thank you!

DR BRÉS. *(To herself)* Merde. Ces homes Anglais; ils n'ont pas l'endurance. Pah! *(Damn – these English men, they have no stamina.)*

(She considers following him, but then turns and heads up the mountain alone.)

Allez.

(In the garden, the final verse of the song builds the spell to a crescendo. By now the fox, the mouse and any other animals of the garden world join in too.)

Scene Eight

Summer

(Several days later, MRS MEDLOCK *and* MRS PHIPPS *are doing household jobs in a room, when* MARTHA *bursts in.)*

MARTHA. Mrs Medlock, Mrs Medlock, he's back!

MRS PHIPPS. Lord above, keep tha voice down.

MRS MEDLOCK. Who's back?

MARTHA. Mr Craven.

MRS MEDLOCK. It's not possible.

MRS PHIPPS. But we're not ready for him!

MRS MEDLOCK. He can't be back. He's gone for a month.

MARTHA. But I saw a carriage.

MRS MEDLOCK. You saw the Doctor.

MARTHA. It's not the doctor.

MRS MEDLOCK. Martha Sowerby, Mr Craven is not back and will not be back for weeks. And praise the Lord for if he only knew –

MR CRAVEN. *(Bursting in)* Where's my son?

(Panic. A sudden wave of stumbling into curtseys.)

MRS MEDLOCK. Mr Craven! Sir –

MR CRAVEN. Where's my son? I went to his room and he's not there!

MRS MEDLOCK. But he must be, the doctor's to come to see him.

MR CRAVEN. He's not there. And his calipers were on the floor and his chair was empty. What have you done with him, woman?

MRS MEDLOCK. Sir, I've done my best. It's that meddlesome girl.

MR CRAVEN. What?!!

MRS MEDLOCK. *(Tearfully)* I did all I could but she's unstoppable.

MARTHA. I know where he is, Sir.

MR CRAVEN. You? Do you, child?

MRS MEDLOCK. I'm sure she doesn't.

MARTHA. He's in the garden. The Secret Garden.

MR CRAVEN. What? !

*(**MR CRAVEN** is off. The others follow.)*

*(Cut to the garden. **BEN** is trimming the hedges. The lamb and fox are gamboling about, the robin is flitting and Mr Wildeebeast is following **MARY** as usual. The children are playing an Indian game. **COLIN** 's crutches lie to one side. He's now walking normally.)*

COLIN. My turn, my turn to seek.

*(**DICKON** strides over to him with the blindfold.)*

Wait! I want Mary to put my blindfold on.

MARY. What do you say?

COLIN. Please.

*(**MARY** blind folds him. He raises his arms to start the game.)*

COLIN. 'Ubho ubho nai chhe!'

(Then they take his hands and they walk in a ring together chanting. (This is a rhyme about an elephant and the sound it makes))

ALL THREE.
'LAAMBI SUNDHH VAADU MATHU LAINE,
DHAM DHAM KARTO JAA CHHE,
SUPADI JEVA KAAN HALAAVI
UBHO UBHO NAI CHHE.'

MARY. See if you can find us! Ben, don't say anything!

BEN. Right you are then.

(They then spin **COLIN** *around once, then* **MARY** *and* **DICKON** *run off and hide in the greenery out of sight.* **COLIN** *sets off, arms outstretched trying to find them.)*

(Then **MR CRAVEN** *enters the garden, almost falling into it he is in such a hurry, followed by the rest of the ensemble. He is about to kick off when he notices the little boy, blindfolded, walking without crutches. He stops in his tracks.* **COLIN** *moves towards him. The others, entering, witness this.)*

COLIN. Mary? Dickon?

*(***MR CRAVEN** *walks slowly towards* **COLIN.** *As he gets closer the servants look on and* **MARY** *and* **DICKON** *come out from their hiding places.* **COLIN** *gets to* **MR CRAVEN,** *who kneels down.* **COLIN** *touches his face, and is momentarily confused until he realises.)*

MR CRAVEN. Colin?

COLIN. Father? *(Removing his blindfold)* Father!

(They embrace.)

MR CRAVEN. You can walk? You're not sick?!

COLIN. We did magic. Look! Look!

*(***COLIN** *stands and jumps, then runs (for the first time) round the periphery of the garden, back into his father's arms.)*

MR CRAVEN. I can't believe it. How is it possible?

COLIN. Mary made me better. And Dickon. And the garden.

MR CRAVEN. Mary? Mary, come here.

(MARY holds back. She doesn't know if she's in trouble or not.)

You broke into the garden, when you knew it was forbidden. You stole your way in, and came in here, all by yourself. And did this? You are a very, very...precious little girl. *(He hugs MARY)* Your parents would be so proud of you. And you Dickon, thank you. Though – what on earth have you done to my dog?

(The dog enters, happy and giddy with friendliness. He runs straight up to MRS MEDLOCK and gives her a slobbery kiss, almost knocking her over. She finds him revolting.)

You have thawed his ice. And mine. And my little boy, my little broken boy – *(to COLIN)* look at you now.

MRS MEDLOCK. But the doctor said! And we believed him. He told us to keep him out of the light, strapped to his bed.

MR CRAVEN. Mrs Medlock...

MRS MEDLOCK. *(Almost weeping)* I always wanted what was best for him, Sir, I really did, I just did what I was told.

MR CRAVEN. I know you did. You are a good woman. There's only one person to blame in this and by God we will hold him to account.

(Doctor Craven enters. He doesn't realise that MR CRAVEN is there.)

DR CRAVEN. Mrs Medlock, I couldn't find you anywhere, but – *(seeing COLIN)* What on earth? Are you mad?! Why is he outside! Colin, get back inside! Cover him up. Quickly! This fresh air will be the death of him.

MR CRAVEN. I don't think that's true, is it cousin?

(Archibald's dog begins to growl.)

DR CRAVEN. Archie. I didn't know you were here.

MR CRAVEN. You kept my boy weak and sickly...for what? The house? The land? The money?

DR CRAVEN. I can explain –

MR CRAVEN. Get out.

DR CRAVEN. If you'll just let me –

MR CRAVEN. I'll see you spend the rest of your years in prison, if it's the last thing I do. Now get out. Out! And never come back! *(To the dog)* Get him!

(The dog lurches at him. The Doctor high tails it out at speed. Everyone is overjoyed, except MARY.)

MR CRAVEN. Mary, what's wrong?

MARY. What about the garden? What will happen to it now? Will you lock it up again?

MR CRAVEN. Never. Never ever. Mary, you brought it back to life. You brought us all back to life. We'll keep the garden open, and everyone will be free to walk here and play here, and we'll keep it wild, so birds can nest here, and everything can grow. And whenever a child is sick, or someone is sad, the gate will always be open, and we will bring them here and make them well again.

MARY. Like magic?

MR CRAVEN. Like magic.

(DICKON takes up his pipe and begins to play. Charmed by the song, the animals begin to dance, as if under his spell. A dance. A happy ending.)

(Curtain)

Lightning Source UK Ltd.
Milton Keynes UK
UKHW021145030420
361293UK00005B/125

9 780573 150418